MW00633524

Workers' Compensation

Poems of Labor & the Working Life

by
Jannie M. Dresser

SUGARTOWN PUBLISHING
Crockett, California
2013

© 2013 Jannie M. Dresser

Workers' Compensation
Poems of Labor & the Working Life

Library of Congress Cataloging-in-Publication Data
Application in process

ISBN # 978-0-9882007-7-7

Sugartown Publishing
1164 Solano Ave., #140
Albany, CA 94706
sugartownpublishing.com

Printed by Minuteman Press
Berkeley, CA

Cover and book design by Margaret Copeland
Cover photograph by Michele Scotto, *sequinedasphault.com*
Author's photo by Julian López-Morillas
Interior photos by the author

Table of Contents

In Memory of My Mother,
Deborah Elizabeth Shannon,
who worked so hard for so long
but never forgot to smell
the roses.

Preface

I BEGAN WORK IN THE OLD-SCHOOL WORKING-CLASS WAY. Children were expected to pitch in and help meet the family's daily needs. Cooking, house-cleaning, and yard work were my first jobs.

By age fifteen, I was leaving high school algebra early to bus across town to where my mother worked in an insurance agency office. I learned the rigors of answering phones, running the copy machine, and filing policies.

I cannot count the number of jobs I have worked at since high school. Though I feel lucky to have usually been able to find work, I realize that work has often interfered with other dreams. Tillie Olsen, in her book *Silences* describes how many writers and artists have not been able to produce their life work because they had to earn a living, support families, and meet other responsibilities which often left them exhausted at day's end. I have frequently juggled more than one job while attending college, building a business, or while doing the dance of supporting myself while attempting to preserve a little time and energy for my true passion of poetry.

For all the hours and efforts I and my ancestors have put into work it has never made anyone in my immediate family wealthy. I come from a long line of farmers and tradespeople, seamstresses and bookkeepers, professions generally not known for high earnings. My grandfather lost his farm in the crash of '29; recently, we lost our family home during the real estate and credit crunch of the 2008 recession.

Working-class people have long carried a disproportionate amount of debt and tax burden in American society. Yet, my family would be proud to tell you that they have never taken a government hand-out, and have often resented those who resort to social welfare. Many in my family would not identify themselves as working class. I "got it" that I was working class when my first jobs out of high school were in a fruit-packing house and in a factory that manufactured automobile safety belts.

For some reason, I always felt work was an interesting topic for poems. This is not a book to win poetry prizes: the taste in poetry these days tends toward experimentation or epiphany-driven lyricism.

By contrast, these are gut-level, rather direct language narratives attesting to the daily grind. I offer them in the spirit of poets who feel the need to testify to hard truths and uncomfortable feelings, perhaps even bitch a bit about work, unpleasant bosses, low wages and the whims of the economy. Writing about work is not (usually) sexy; it can carry resentment and bitterness — reader, be forewarned.

I hope you enjoy my poems; may some of them speak to you.

JANNIE M. DRESSER
Crockett, California
Autumn 2013

Better is a handful of gratification
Than two fistfuls of labor which is pursuit of the wind.
— Ecclesiastes 4:6

Farm to Factory

The Packing House

That old Clovis road
smelled of peaches rotting.
Sunrise, driving to work
at the packing house, I watched
mirages loom
in the hot asphalt.
By early afternoon
the thin heat lowered
on the packers
as we stood along the conveyor belt
below a sheet metal roof.

At break Hilda and me
drove to the nearest
irrigation ditch and threw murky water
over our hot shoulders,
then back to stand,
soaking wet in our positions.

The whole day the boss' teenage son
rode around us
in his black Firebird
with red competition stripes.
Sometimes he'd strut by,
order us not to talk.

Late in the day, dry dust
rose from the dirt road
where old cars and pickup trucks
came back from the orchards,
full of men, sweaty from picking,
returning to their shacks
behind the owner's house.

Just past sundown packers went home
raising a cloud above every set of headlights.

We drove past the white pillared mansion,
past the rich green pasture,
past sleek quarter horses grazing,
into a sunset of overripe peaches.

We looked, exhausted, into the evening,
too tired to notice our long dark stream
of old beat up cars.

What the Children Saw

We peeked, each of us with one bare toe
squeezed into a knothole,
glad to trade the pain for another view.

Didn't see trees back there, just
a concrete patio blotched with dirt,
blood, and in the far corner,
heavy wooden crates, bound with baling wire.

Full of rabbits, hundreds of them,
all young ones, hiding in the shadows.

Over their heads a sheet of crinkled metal
stretched across the neighbor's yard.
Underneath, lined up against
the back fence were ten silver buckets.

Catching steady drips from where
they hung, above, their necks wrung out.

Coop

Mrs. Wilson candled eggs in the chicken runs —
our playhouse on summer afternoons.
We girls watched the beam that foretold
was the egg fertile, alive in its whitish shell
        spotted brown.

Sally's family owned the ranch; I dashed
across the county road to a dusty feather
freedom, cute hatchlings spinning under
hot-white lamps: yellow dervishes
        fluttering up, frenzying down.

Our job was scouting nearby fields,
chickens that had gotten out, gotten lost.
We picked a path through puncture vines,
across ditch beds, crushing dirt clods
        underfoot, then running back.

Our small hands grasped gravelly legs
as we stared at downward beaks. We dropped
half-rotted culls down a black hole.
I stood at the edge of its metal lid,
a darkened eye, swaying —

oddly triumphant — as the dead bird brushed
along the cellar walls, scuffling as I breathed
the hellish smell below. It was a magic spell
I felt could keep more country deaths at bay.

Afterwards, Sally and I turned somersaults
in our summer shifts, twirled across the browning
lawn, then twined ourselves in ropes beneath
the sycamore: letting go, we untangled fast,
        jumped at break-neck speed.

Learning from Pioneers

What got left behind were castoff
goods, abandoned graves dissolved
in dust mirage, a house half buried
by sun-caked sod. Digging through
old maps and logs, I've got no trails
to lead me on; my tools are books,
photos, pens; with them I seek
their names, not knowing where
the herds once knelt at edge of day.

I take my lessons from reeds,
tamped-down grass, grain spilt
from canvas sacks, wagon ruts
embossed on hard-packed soil.
They lugged seed in barrels,
the best of what they could bring
from home. I try to do as natives
would: set ear upon the ground,
listen for sounds — grinding wheels
or axle break, the screech of carts
suspended off the sides of cliffs,
dropped to valleys down below.

I linger on the scent of cabin wood,
its smoke a wreath of ghosts curled
in the hearth, the sight of budding
trees in orchard rows. I excavate
the hostile places too, recover what
remains: salt memories, drunken dreams,
grit of tear-washed pain. My ancestors
were strengthened by the heft of metal
tools, made righteous at each hairpin
turn that folded back upon itself,
as they rose and crossed each
impassable muddy mountain road.

Under prairie sky, I'm blinded by
blue-black storms of what has been
lost, with little time to scratch names
deep within a signpost's heart,
etch letters on weathered stones.

From My Perspective

After Edward Hopper's "House by the Railroad" (1926)

You think all there is to see
is my three-story clapboard white
touched by dusk, my orange chimney
reaching its fist toward heaven,
my porch barren as it is, wood
splintered since last spring.

Critics claim me for their solitude,
judging from the far side
of the rust-brown track that races
through slatternly weeds; they theorize
the deep gloaming range, gauge
my rough foundation. Yet, I am
further out than they can imagine.

All settlement, a mansion of
redolent eternity. Within my shades,
rooms darken until they are just
cool memory of day. Candles blaze
silhouettes against papered walls.
Girls once tucked their dolls in beds
covered with white lace and chenille.

Between the hour of set sun and lit
lamps — that is my time. To the east
and west, I listen for cattle grazing,
for the soft Braille of sheep pressing
prairie grasses down. Beyond,
farmhouses are alive, rooftops amber
in vesper light pulsing prairie code.

Out here on the plains, there is no
loneliness, just afternoons and locusts.
My occupants rub their working hands
together, bend down upon their knees
to offer wheat-stained prayers. Between
the hour of set sun and burning lamps,

I take my time. I sigh, walls opening
on each side to a wide American silence.

Those carefully trained to remark
across the distances, they only document
the circumference of their own emptiness,
mistake themselves framing it as mine.

The Field

I went to the field
to eat my bread.
It tasted of yeast;
the sunlight was no
measurable distance.
Absence of coyotes,
rabbits, rats, and
no predatory birds.

All green translucence
as I sat for hours
gumming dough
with my salty tongue,
wondering what waste
was on the world
in her stark bones.
I went to the field,
sat stone still until
dusty midnight
came, his fine finger
tipping off his head.

Alive, alive-oh, he sang.
That brute. I walked
to the valley's cove
where madwomen
bake their bread.
I went from the field
and gave my blood,
gave and gave till a green
light sang in me,
something fierce,
nothing tame.

Potato Salad

Discard skins, root brown reminders
of soil we've left behind.
Cut in half, drop spuds
in cold salt water, a pan
wide enough for boiling.
Turn the heat up, cover (not completely).
Boil ten minutes till soft —
not over soft. Let the pan's round rim
grow thick with spud-white
settled foam.

Cut steaming chunks
into a heavy ceramic bowl, grate
onions through oval holes,
scrape 'til fingers burn. Your eyes
not fit for anything but tears.
Add mayonnaise, slivered hard-boiled
eggs, sprinkle one-fourth cup
of pickle juice, the sweetened
kind. Add sharp dried mustard,
a pinch or more, olives chopped —
the tangs of taste you crave.

Leave room for eccentricity,
more mayonnaise. Scoop mayonnaise
by creamy spoonfuls.
Lick the wooden spatula.
Oil is good. Potatoes are good.
Families are good. Serve warm,
cold, or in between; eat heartily.
Smack your lips together.
Repeat out loud: "I wonder
what the poor are eating
for dinner tonight . . . wonder
what the poor . . . eat . . .
tonight."

Fresno Suite

Summer
Mexican farmers
lean by roadsides.
Tan Impalas coated
in vineyard dust.
One old man's hand
sifts dead air,
settles on raisins
snug in folded brown
paper packets.
Peaches drop
one by one.
Nectarines, aching plums
plunk and splat
before a flat horizon.
Mirages followed hard
by water drawn
from a nearby ditch.

Autumn
Brown shoes scrape
against the front porch steps,
worn thick layers:
dry earth, mud,
summer's ending.
Down Blackstone, a flatbed truck
hauls wine-skinned onions
to market. Some slip
between wood pallets
piled high, raw sweet bursts
on hot asphalt
in Indian summer.
Cotton-heavy,
the back of a man slumps
in a dining chair,
wishes he didn't have to face
another day.
Memories fold over and over
in late slant light.

Winter
Hawks return
through southern lowlands.
Beneath frost-bit fields,
rodents scratch
themselves to sleep.
Oranges dot dark green
orchards in remembrance
of summertime.
If it doesn't kill them,
a final chill
sweetens best.

Spring
Walking to school,
umbrellas opened,
we warmed our hands
inside Christmas muffs.
On rain-moist asphalt,
the potched road bears
starburst universes
in drops of oil.
Fruit orchards float
over irrigation moats.
Around trunks of white-washed
trees, a skin of mud.
And overhead, the branches
ready their escape
from regimental rows,
lifting darkening green
into an open field
of April sky.

The Sound of Another Language

I was walking beside a river.
I needed to cross.
There were vines hanging
        from tall spirited trees.
Everything was golden-lit, burnished browns,
        the dampness and mulch
        of late fall afternoons.
Fields to my left with workers bent
        speaking in another tongue.

I continued to walk along this dark river
        needing to cross; a panther
Like blackest night, like an iron pan,
        like Charon in his craft,
This panther drew up to me, then stretched himself:
        long body on a tree's bright limb.
I slipped onto his back, gripped around
        felt the round hard smoothness —
Panther belly under my fingers.

We swam the river. On the wild cat's back
        I rode, my feet bare,
        touching coolness of water.
I crossed the river. On the other side
        the panther was soaked.
He shook himself, the way cats do,
        then sizzled into air —
        a wisp of smoke
Then silence.

Farm Workers Line Up for Calisthenics

Just past dawn and the *campesinos* warm up,
circled off the dusty side
of Highway 99.
They execute deep-knee bends, shoulder rolls,
a grove-side yoga I'm surprised to see.

In bandanas, blue jeans, red flannel shirts
and orchard-ready shoes,
they look like some lost tribe of Man,
dressed to recognize each other, or perhaps,
warriors preparing for battle.

Here on the valley floor —
flat as a sheet of steel, where goods are pressed
to pallets — there are only rows:
bright greens, tomatoes, walnut trees.
Magic fruits and fields ripe for
late season harvesting.

They will pack the best of them
in baskets bound for winter's place:
Michigan, Vermont,
points in the farthest East
where a sunny orange
is the greatest gift on New Year's Day,

a promise the world will grow
beyond the fall of man, saved
not by an injured God,
but by a worker's steady grace.

La Migra

The fence is crowned with small badges
of broken soda bottles,
sharp against any who would climb the night
who might crawl over
to clean, to haul, to pick, to peel, to bend.
Badges that once shined
like tiny *estrellas* are now dim under dust.
The hired men stack bricks,
ladle mortar — masons too hurried to scrape
the excess, busily
constructing another wall, one to separate
a fine hotel
and the *mercado de artesanias*, the market
where hands bleed
for work, the chance to leap into a night sky
full of our Milky Way,
the *camino de leche*
to America where we pay *la migra muchas dolares*
of green leaves banded
in red, money we pour into walls, into borders
to hold back tradition,
the migrants of time. When shall we ever cross,
cross over and over,
hands gloved in thick leather, our brown hands,
our white hands,
that could reach, fly over *la migra* like wings
rising above these
mute ramparts in *corridos* of song?

Chile Relleno

It is a bit like love: a green heart
bathed in the blood of an orange lamb
set before me by Chula. I know her
by her hands and her smile,
by an apron trimmed in red rick-rack.
Back before days of serving trays,
there was a kitchen with wood cupboards,
freshly wiped counters, and other women
who open packages bursting with chilies,
wide as green hearts, in order to take
each to a countertop and pound it,
then coat it with yellow meal and orange
queso. But even before them there was
a man driving a flatbed truck piled
with cartons, turning onto the road
to town at dawn or at dusk, and black oil
was burned to make that truck run.
The man works hard; I'm sure of it,
and at home has a wife with her share
of woes and of corn. She knows the farmer
who grows chilies far out in high desert;
she knows his wife who daily draws
water from stones. And on the hillside,
there's a dairy where cows circle
in the barnyard driving dust down
as they turn the queso in their bovine
warmth, queso for the dinner
of a woman who exchanges dollars
for pesos, dollars she has earned
somewhere chilies can't grow.

Deportees

My dad drove the deportation truck
down the valley. It wasn't a summer
job or regular profession but what
he could get between drunken jags.

Hauling deportees to Tijuana, perhaps
he lorded it over them out of shame,
his own migrant manhood. Or, maybe,
he enjoyed their company, was friendly,
apologetic, seeing them as hard-working
the way he had been hard-working
once — when he could steady himself
to lift the hammer, mark nails cleanly
into wooden seams. I hope he joined
in singing some *corridos*, drank their
tequila in hot sun verging the range
of mountains east of Bakersfield
or at desert stops along the Salton Sea.

August was a beat month souring peaches,
a dizzying insistence of crop dusters,
helicopters out to spot the aliens. Maybe,
he simply prayed for home along side
his busload of hot Mexicans — halfway
between plucked fruit and yards full
of laughing kids somewhere, back where
all had been left fatherless at home.

Tapete

Mr. Fernandez's family
weaves carpets to sell.
His shop arrays
rugs on every table,
they spill from every
corner, cover every wall,
counter, shelf.
Muchos colores zing —
azul, blanco, rosa, marrón.

I have walked into
a kaleidoscope.
If only I could buy them all —
the prices are reasonable —
I would carry Mexico
back with me to my
young grey country.

San Joaquin Equinox

From the grey-tint window of our passing train,
I anticipate the sweetness of summer corn;
it is early spring and our valley has reverted
to marsh. We're migrants, up and down
the tracks, stopping to scout among the tules,
turn eyes on new-plowed rows. Here a planter
has placed a rose bush at the head of his vineyard.

The orchards green and lush, they color the sky
all the way to the foothills and the false horizons:
thick black branches — walnut trees, almonds, figs —
hold winter in stiff regard, shadows shortening
beneath their limbs; redwing blackbirds fledging
to form small silhouettes along the power grid.

Through the valley towns, the full length
of our passing train reflects in sliding doors,
plate-glass set in flimsy aluminum sidings.
Tract-home yards buried under weeds, scattered
toys, half-dug holes of lazy hounds, machines
abandoned to soil and rust, broken jungle gyms.

Even the junkyards are cast off in some scornful
disregard: jalopies piled side-by-side
the rain-washed fields. Perhaps their puddles
sprout new life, tadpoles waiting to become
frogs among fallen twigs. One hubcap sticks
out from the muddied road; catching settled light,
it looks like some mutant thing that wants to grow.

Fruit Stand

Off Chestnut, the dirt road takes you back
and a man comes from the other side
of the darkened screen door, one arm pinched
up from polio, the other full of strength
enough to sack each chosen fruit after
he weighs it on a beat-up silver scale.

His black-brown hound pulses in the heat
under a sycamore, the chain wrapped
around tan bark. He's past his time
of shooting after car-wheels, fails
to bark at your approach.

The peaches were unlike any you'd ever
bought at the grocery store: rose-rinsed,
softball-sized, sweet as marshmallow;
you can hardly wait to take one bite,
to suck yesterday's warm arc
of sunshine.

As summer gathers itself under the long
San Joaquin afternoons, you find
black plums, nectarines, tomatoes
red as fingers cut and sore, soft
in their meat.

All you can say to the man whose name
you've never asked,
who grunted more
than spoke, was
thank you,
      thank you,
           thank you.

Point Judith

Fish, chips, and ale. We settle in for our unintended wait,
for the mechanic to open shop at dawn,
caught out by winter's bitter two-step — snow and ice,
snagged by that metal claw covered under
a foot of snow, guarding the entrance to the hotel's
back lot. I tried warning you ('don't back up!')
when I saw the sign, then heard our tire blow.
It goes that way in winters on Narragansett Bay.

It's not really such a hardship — to be thrown off
our tourist's course, nothing compared
to what these fishermen endure. We watch,
comfy, secure and warm, in our red naugahyde
booth, white breath fogging plate-glass
in the dock-dive as midnight nears.

Just below, fearless gulls criss-cross the shallow air
above a trawler where two men hoist supplies.
Ice layers inches thick on deck so the smaller man
in yellow rubber boots blasts water
from a heavy hose while his buddy pushes
a six-foot broom across the planks.

My God, they look so cold: no gloves, no heavy coats,
bare hands drawing up a fist-round rope,
the anchor. We watch as they pull out
toward Atlantic swells and distant lobster shoals
where herring gulls patrol the churning stream
the way they've done so many times before.

The Andrea Gail, 1991

After watching "The Perfect Storm" and for George Dresser
lost out of Gloucester.

When Captain says "We might make it out," we sense the giddy
serenity that comes with finally having turned the boat. The lull
arrives; there's a certainty we'll survive; can almost taste
its taffy pink stretched by patient hands. Grand illusion dulls
all fear: searchlight dazzling off a voluminous screen. But,
movie fans, life isn't like that — our skeleton mast snaps in half —
a toothpick cracked by Poseidon's roiling surf. That sunburst
across the boom is the last, bright Tantalus of hope; one moment
more and the clouds darken into a gummy licorice, the likes
of which we've never seen — shadows all: the boat, the crew.
Captain says "She won't let us out." Then the cabin window
bursts beneath the awesome wave; we climb again the monster's
back, rage until we're flipped, sucked down. How close we came,
how truly hard we fought.

Sixteen Tons

A man holds the rein looped over the mule.
The mule carries diamonds from the mine.

All day in its cage, the yellow canary chirps.
The deeper into the pit, the more to extract.

The inner sanctum is overcome by smoke;
memory is a pine-wood chair that rocks
on an empty porch.

The mule coughs and sputters in its byre.

Men's faces a mile down the color of coal;
the feathered yellow bird has ceased to breathe.

Sugartown

For my adopted hometown of Crockett, California

The old brick factory senses the tide: water mixing
with other water, salt, tules, old tires that squat
along the sludgy shore.

The view is hillwise to skyline; wild turkeys
amble midday streets and ubiquitous raccoons
cadge garbage can meals.

The elusive fox trots under dim lamps. We have
rose-munching deer, assaulting jays, vultures
kettling estuarial updrafts.

When the hustle was on, Hawaii sent its cane;
the San Joaquin flooded Port Costa with boxcars:
sorghum, barley, wheat and beets.

Houses built like stevedores, some ramshackle now,
are two-story studios for retirees, artists,
others who want the city at arm's length.

The refinery nearby lets out a leak and we smell
sulfur for a night. Who cares? Train whistles,
our only noise, except for endless talk
from old-timers
fading fast.

Factory Poem

In my town we refined sugar cane
and oil, we made white crystals
of brown stalks and black rivers
of earth's rust.

We had signal towers, tall as *Tour Eiffel,*
labyrinths of clanging rooms
to befuddle any wayward Theseus.
We had goals in sight, bins to fill.

Around the brick-and-mortar factory,
white minarets rose from fire-breathing crows.

There were dwellings from which workers
sallied forth in four-by-fours, jalopies, pick-up
trucks who turned into the gate, flashing
magic plastic badges to claim their place.

For cooperating with the powers that were
(captains of fading industry), we got a city
park, funding for the school, band uniforms.
Maybe higher cancer rates came too,
an occasional toxic spill.

We got a night sky lit by graveyard shifts:
explosion of white against a faded
midnight tapestry.

Now, our country's stars are out of work;
all they do is blast pristine, aimless light.

Trenton Makes, The World Takes

Wherever you grew up, there comes a day when the sign
across the bridge leading you back to your hometown
reveals its tragic truth as you show it off to someone
you've just met, someone from somewhere else.

That's when you see it through other eyes: cold and sober,
unfiltered by nostalgia. That's when the pride of being
a hometown prodigal, the one who got away, made it big,
sifts out like smoke, and you are stung by the grand slam of it.

We are always leaving home; still we ache when the home
team fails. What keeps us looking back through a misted lens,
shoring up memories of the once-that-was — even as we jump
on bandwagons, leap into the unexpected run?

Trenton wears her faded crown from when manufacturer
was king — maven of schools, hospitals, and city hall.
On the bridge, her diadem reflects the river; "the world takes"
sons and daughters, every damn thing she used to make.

Overhead

Suspended on a metal catwalk held aloft
by steel threads, the pair of bird-men
go about this foggy San Francisco day,
doing their hammering, plying their trade:
an eight-hour exchange of time and labor.

Another building climbs to the dreadful sky,
dreamed up in other buildings
like the one they build now, by thinkers
in offices, cubicles, the plans scribed
in profit-and-loss statements, rough proposals,
blueprints faxed to financiers.

Down below, I raise my eyes to the
lowest paid captains of industry, the builders
themselves who take their risks
the way true men should: outside
on high-slung scaffolding where birds perch,
puzzled by the hard-hatted intruders.

We all wonder how they survive, day
after day dangling on the sides of half-built
monoliths, like those ancient hewers
and hefters of standing stones, like
the slaves and peasants who hoisted
up the pyramids of kings.

Lowell

I
You can call me Betsy, Harriet, or Louisa.
In truth, I come before you,
anonymous though recorded in industrial lore.
I come to Lowell in 1844, been working
cotton five years, maybe more.
Send money home.
I buy my own way, pay at the boarding house,
get my hats and confections
after sending brother to school,
paying dad's farm debt.
Charles Dickens came to read to us, praised
our white clothes, still soft cheeks.
Emerson extolled us to reach
for higher things.
But, it is the trill of birds, the echo
of the lolling brook I miss.
Standing here in the factory door,
watching the sun retreat, I hear
looms scrape the rolls of cloth. Such is
the price of our refinement.

II
Tying up ends, I live all day under
the spinning jenny. Threads break
over head, thunder sounds, foreman shouts:
"Taut threads! Break outs! Tie ups."
Uncle backs away,
one heavy shoe pressing down.
He backs to the far wall,
pulls cotton onto bobbins off of spools,
gets some distance; then I scoot
below the avalanche,
pretty water-colored threads.
An under stream sprays cotton fibers;
got to keep things moist to work 'em.
One line busts loose: I dash between
the jerky engine and uncle's blackened boots,

tie it up fast before the loom
crashes back: waves banging
into threads, threads pounding into cloth.
We don't want loose ends in this factory.
That's why they keep me here,
out of school, out of harm's way.

Poe At Lowell (1846)

After the seven o'clock blow-out,
the factory lanterns ceased, after
the twelve-hour ear-drum splitting day,
looms and bobbin spun in constant
whir-whiz. . . after supper with Susan,
Rebecca, Mary, the other country girls,
we gather late to hear the Master
in black velvet robes and haunted smell,
with his dark moustache and regal air.

We take our seats, row-behind-row,
a crest of white bonnets, rough hands
prim on muslin laps. We still our thumbs
from the twelve-hour throb of labor
wrested on our bones; wait patiently
for gaslights dimmed, a moment's lull,
to quiet the tintinnabulation in our ears.
He begins, *Once upon a midnight dreary*
while I pondered weak and weary,
Over many a quaint and curious
volume of forgotten lore. Melody to rival
a darker angel's forgotten nature,
music to quiet our dull limbs.

We succumb to his sweet madness:
go wherever the poem will take us.
Close our eyes, swallow breaths
down our chilled throats. For an hour
he sang: *Open here I flung the shutter,*
when with many a flirt and flutter,
In there stepped a stately Raven
of the saintly days of yore. Weight
of spinning jennies lifted: all mill girls
wear those grinding stones or coats of chain
that roar and trip us up inside the looms.

But the poet takes us to the land
where a black bird's chant
that *Nevermore* thrills, brightens,
warms our pale souls. Next day,
in giggles or disdain, we say —

one girl to t'other — that "nevermore"
repeating, "nevermore," brightening
the sun-dark day. Where our windows
do not open we fill the panes
with pages pasted from our Bibles
or poems we'll come to know, yellowed right
through papers, like sun itself, such
astonishments and wonders waiting
at close of day, beyond our rough
cobblestones, the brickyard gate.

Sprung

This summer, I will not be working
for U.S. Safety Corporation building
you a better seat belt. I'll no longer
twist the long black tongues of stiff
nylon thread through a Plexiglas™
shock-box filled with gears and levers,
to snap each into place. It was my job
to check for resistance, chuck the ones
that didn't lock into the red cart,
the others in the green. Good luck.

You won't find me taking my stand
with the rest of the girls, our hair tied
in braids, buns or wrapped in scarves,
our hands circling above coiled springs
popping across conveyor belts before
we could dab the thick brown grease
into each: guarantee for smoother wind-
up and release. (In case of accident: pray.)

This is one damn summer I won't
shout over busted machinery, or keep
my brown-bag lunch off the equipment,
on the floor; I won't miss the red-haired
foreman telling us *"Knock the small talk off!"*
watch him — my mouth gone numb —
fire the black guy with no explanation.
I'll miss farewell picnics on the sunbaked
blacktop lot because I'm no longer one
of the girls. You won't catch me
slacking in my used Nova day after day-loud
day, rolling the window down, cranking
the A.M. high as she'll go. There is no safety
strap in my car for the long drive home.

This summer, the only time clock I'll have
to punch is that dull grey box that keeps
rattling its tick-tick-tick inside my head.

Pig Iron

for Diane Wang

Some put their hand in the fire, call it
'beautiful,' a goddess that makes industry
holy and what we are: to work
as a maker, to be willing to become
one with the raw materials rushing
toward cohesion as a perfect new form.
You standing in the path of molten steel,
alive in full body gear, awestruck.
The liquid metal cascading from the cauldron.
If it were a dream I would have
interpretations, would pose variations.
But this is, was your real willingness
to interpose your young self as a part
of the process even Hephestia and Vulcan
were doing in those mythic days.
The steel trembling from its orange-red
bowl of flame, reflects in the goggles
and whooshes into my own imagination
as you tell your story of work long ago.
We took strange jobs in our twenties:
your path as an industrial worker of the world,
my path as a poet in the making.
Zorba the Greek said 'to live is to
take off your belt and dance.' He never
mentioned the belt was bronze heavy
and cut from the leg. Still,
this is a good message, as good as one gets,
something to aspire toward with all your will
and heart. We have worked in the world,
received our injuries and pay cuts, profited
in the only way we could, with stories
to tell and shields and swords to hone
fine as anything that comes from baser metals.

Assembly Line I

They look different than the vibrating rubber mats
of yesteryear
Now our cubicles catch up to us
surrounded by chilling beige, dull greys
We speak all day to digits
Thumbing our fingers like iconoclastic monkeys
Being given yet another
Ladder rung to prove how inescapably free we are
Tied to these schedules and machines
The watched clock torn down
Off the wall, the windows sealed
In vast canopied rooms
We no longer need bosses
We have become our own best time-motion sensor
Each time we pick up the ringing phone
Step away from our computers
Like magic, we disappear into air
Into thin temperature-controlled
Blood-stained air.

Assembly Line II

I've broken up a
lotta jams working on assembly lines. Rolling trays
on little
wheels snag against each
other, lock up, block the ever-moving forward
of peaches,
plums, little nectarines. And
in stores, I clerked and had to shake
up, break
up lines of customers
all on the edge of buying,
something that would ease
their minds.
I've punched out
cash register buttons like mad, and rang
them all up with a smile,
bagging each purchase, saying
thank you so much.
Co-workers and I made a game of
passing as many through
in minimum time. But every deadline
has its vulnerabilities:
back-ups, log-jams,
tandem random side-tracks.
You might see this as the problem of
the time-space
continuum: lines running on
parallel tracks, never quite reaching that point when
they are
supposed to come together,
or you might just call it
capitalism's
butterfly effect.

Saturday Night

The one time sanctioned by the secular world
to stand inviolate between two days off work.
That's why we need to light the candles,
spread the cornstarch across the patio,
or put the speakers out the back windows,
or tell the neighbors to come on over,
or set out that kettle of fried fish,
or put on the best pair of dancing shoes.

The one time sanctioned by the secular world
when to party is to celebrate life and love,
when the car with a red rose rolls up,
when your stockings get torn,
when you lose your virginity,
when you stay out way too late.

It's for making trouble, making whoopie, making
good on those six days of sweat and taking it,
taking the grief of a mean boss,
taking the tedium of a tan cubicle,
taking the dissatisfaction of customer service,
taking the rhythm of the time clock, the notary
stamp, the fifth signature sealing the deal,
taking the stir of the twizzle stick and the sickly
taste of fake sugar, taking cremora
and doughnuts and co-workers'
birthdays or baby showers, meetings
that drone on in some manager's
small but imperious tone.

The one time sanctioned by the secular world:
the secular world's remedy for emptiness,
our accommodation for taking the very
life blood from you all throughout,
during, enduring the rest of that
unholy commercial week.

Bone Tired

I keep saying, 'I'm tired,' knowing
that saying it perpetuates the feeling.
Exhaustion is different. It's bone tired
I keep saying. The droopy lid, low
blood sugar, two p.m. tired of having
the daytime settle into lists.

Don't get me wrong. This is no *kvetch*.
It's simply worker tired. There is
a far distance between what I am
and what my ancestors sweated out:
a farmer, a builder, a seamstress,
a hardy Southern wife; they knew
work. This poem is for them.

My tired poem. It'll fold up; I'll put it
in my pocket, roll it into a worry
stone — with the grime of soil,
patina of my tired oily hands.
Will they accept these thanks?
If I complain 'I'm tired,' they'll smile,
nod and tell me: keep your hand
upon the plow, hold on, hold on.

Builders & Makers

Maker of Wooden Nails

I squat on a burlwood bench to begin.
The poor have gathered great branches of wood.
The poor have brought fallen branches.
I give them a coin for redemption,
A coin for a winter coat while all day
I cut large limbs into smaller,
Cut pieces I can work into corners:
This oak or pine, this yew or ash.

I turn the wood on the lathe, scrape
Earth from the bark, bark from the heart
Of the deeper wood, its core —
The nugget we seek where the age
Is told in the wood-heart, where a smooth
Shape grows and strengthens in my hand:
The very thing to marry plane with plane,
Board with bigger board, the best plank
Brought in a kiss of wood to make a house,
A chest as high as a man, a box the size
Of the man's wife for her resting bed.

I squat on a burlwood branch to begin.

Our Houses

After Hopper's "Cape Cod Evening" (1939)

We believed in our houses.
They stood for something —
well-deserved vacations
a stone's throw from the beach.

We kept the woods at bay,
a swirl in their long black
distances. We plied cloud-white paint
thick on clapboard, strained
cans of paint, boarded
storm windows, groomed
our lawns, the collie.

That settling sun still wades
through inevitable dusk,
overgrown grass. The forest
seemed fantastically safe,
where it ceased abruptly
at the edge of yards gone awry;
the harbor we thought was a lake
was dredged to take away time.

Like lace doilies we tried pressing
down, we wanted the dust
to stay in its place. Now,
there's much to do, cross arms
at elbows, pray. In late stage green,
we watch, measuring how
our husbands no longer command
even the dog.

House Painter

I imagined him in rooms
across town, rooms with baseboards
coated twice and window frames
that opened wide to fern grottoes,
rose-lined walks, wisteria topping
a balustrade.

All day I imagined him climbing
paint-speckled ladders,
then his descent; could picture him
scrape window casings,
taping glass. Knew the way
he measured paint in buckets
lined up in steady rows.

My father blended pastel shades
so thick and rich. Full of plans,
he was full of intent, each dipstick
carefully swatched.
Mom's discarded hose caught
impurities, thick clumps
in lead-based oils.

He made those rooms look perfect,
smooth, forever. At dinnertime, I watched
the hands that craved the bar,
the Ivory soap, slumped in a dish
beside the chipped kitchen sink.
Watched his tired, watery stare
strained beyond the backyard
bound by fruitless oleanders,
the splintered fence
always in need of stain.

Fresno, 1960

She sat all day in her father's car
while our dads worked
on the roof next door, up there for hours
in their white coveralls,
nailing shingles, gauging angles:
the black man helping
my southern dad who said 'nigger'
only when he was drunk; otherwise,
he said any man was his equal
when they worked side-by-side
on battlefield or rooftop,
or mixing, lifting paint.

From inside the darkened house,
I cracked the drawn drapes
keeping summer out, to watch her,
wondering to make a new friend.
On the second day, I brought her
to the porch to share lemonade
and dolls but I can't say why
I never invited her inside.

There the swamp cooler blasting
chilled the air; my mom was somewhere
in the back but I don't remember
asking if I could bring my new
acquaintance in. Instead, we played
on the concrete step where ivy
overtook the arch; we sat beside
the weedy lawn for hours and played.

Then one day, she was gone —
her father paid — and I was alone
again yet changed by the girl
without a name, who wore her hair

in pigtails like my own and shared
her doll as I shared mine. For those
few days, our dolls, it seemed,
had welcomed homes.

Dead Battery

The white ship of an old Victorian rises
behind a tar truck.

Stuck in my old car, my battery dead,
I'm waiting for a tow.

I watch the long muscled arms of four men:
three brothers and their father.

They are painting the house across the street
against a spring-blue sky.

Reaching into a tree from the portico, the elder
wears paint-splattered coveralls,

picks kumquats, delicately rubbing each
against his chest.

Then, he tosses them down, each to each.

The men take their turn to ascend
the twenty-foot ladder to the roof,

take their portion of golden fruit, completely
unaware that their paint cans

are splashing brightest blue
onto my careworn day.

Wayne's Left Finger

For my brother on his 55th birthday

Like wounds of war, work leaves its trace —
no purple heart given though, these scars
are etched in risen wall and lowered roof.

Bits of ourselves are left in sod; roads
we've walked demand their tolls. What's left
behind is often small: a restless night,
a lung, my brother's finger tip.

Our limbs are easiest prey — sparrows
on winter twigs. Long hair can be stayed
in nets to protect from grinding gears,
boots laced up tight to keep the ankles strong
but watch those fingers and those toes.

I've had no injury on the job as bad as yours.
Unlike trophies and awards that gather
dust on mantels, take up living space,
hard work's sacrifice is in the solid beam,
the switch that works at night to light a room.

Marks sustained on flesh — the twist of back,
the cough, a swollen leg — remind us:
how a saw can slip, the ladder fall.

Jackhammer

It's not the days of breaking up sidewalk,
the spike pounding thick concrete
that does him in.

I would think the loud vibrations
were the source of spinal
injury, but he tells me no,
it's the lifting.

I look at my brother across the table
in my mother's mobile home
where we digest Thanksgiving
dinner.

In his wedding pictures from years
ago, he was a kid, setting off
to lift life like some two-by-four,
then shave it down.

After these meals, where we laugh
and talk and rib the other's politics,
or change the subject,

I am feeling we have both been caught
by something we aren't
so certain of:

A jackhammer, the piece
of nail that flipped into his eye
while on a job.

I tally my own accounts, how
each year's ruptures mount up
to littler breaks:

my broken appendix,
another troublesome used car.

Perhaps, work is simply
for reducing all our debts,
repaving our bosses'
remodeled homes.

We may vote differently, Wayne and I.
But there's still one hammer
pounding us both down
into well-worn nails
as we hang on to the plank we walk
together, staring off
into our separate empty space.

What's It For?

When a grown man obliterates
his O-gauge train set, every bit
— the mountains sculpted
from papier-mâché and painted
lake (ochre, mossy green, sky-blue),
the small towns laid on the plain,
tiny Victorian houses manifesting
joy and sorrow, small ghosts
tucked into imaginary beds, roads,
the tracks that go 'round and around —
we know then his dream's been
met at its terminus, unwelcome
reality has moved in. My brother
describes his epiphany: After
surveying mocked-up lands
stretching from the wide fake sea
to mustard and heather brae —
covered in garage dust — he
took measure of his disinterest,
its disuse, hours spent those
afternoons that didn't amount
to much. Whether he set it afire
or took pic-axe or shovel to hand,
I don't know. But I do know:
it can be dangerous to ask
"What's it for?" — A whistle blows
soft in the tunnel at night, beyond
range of our hearing, our need
to set time by signals and that
chucka-chucka-chucka
intolerable refrain we fear.
"What's it for?"each day digging
our ditches, laying down track.

Log Roller

It doesn't bother me there is no working ground
under my boot-bred feet; my days are spent
leaping between logs, falling in.

We are a people thrown off by too-thick roots,
prefer the tree brought down, sawed into rough-
cut loops coursing rain and drought.

Clearers of soil, we sold pine for barrels,
traded oak for oil, turned elders into boxcars
then traveled further on.

I'm the one who finally settled down, found
meager success. For this job, you only need
two things: a jacket, thick rubber boots.

Everything else is up to tides to carry forests
down to salt-water mills. You can count
the days in decibels of crushing wood.

So, when you ask, I'll tell you, it don't
bother me there is no ground upon these
brown and barren hills;

I'll never miss those owls who hide in trees
and come out nights to preach
their sorry-assed oaths.

Branches

The boy was pinned under it.
He was breathing but barely.
The men came shouting through the forest.
They had a saw and a rope and an old rag.
It was the cloth that caught
The eye of the deer watching from a pine break.
Red and wounded, clipped by deadfall
Below the moonbranch. It had seen
The tree lurch and crush
Through the wood as if giving chase.
The boy who once climbed to its topmost branch,
Who raided the bird's nest,
Now empty, now scattered:
Twigs askew shocked from the hand
Of the bentbacked boy now downed.

Above, the patient merlin halts
a female sparrow's flight in one
sure quick dive.

Commuter Rooter

His slender hand dangles daintily
from the window on the driver's side.

We had stopped at this red light
when his hand caught my eye.

I'd like to shape its replica in bronze
or marble, were I a sculptor:

fingers narrow, gently long, dropped
easily like stems of pale flowers.

His casual white-shirtsleeve is rolled back
revealing a patient wrist.

Nothing else of him is exposed
in the dreary light at this busy
intersection —

just this perfect gathering, fingers lightly
tapping the outside of his van,

the van advertising the best
rooter plumber in town.

I cannot help imagining where his hands
have been, the muck he has plunged them
into up to the high part of his sleeve.

I send a quiet thank you — not only for his calling —
(we all must use his service now and then)
but for the beauty of his hand, its ability

to fly free from labor like a bride's bouquet
tossed full of immaculate roses into
the cleanest air.

Putting an Old Man to Shame

The printer helped me move cartons of legal journals,
coated in dust; he wore a faded blue work shirt,
khaki pants, and the way men do in their late sixties,
when they are rough-lived and winded, he carried
a handkerchief to frequently wipe his head, clear
the sweat. A lifetime spent behind the clang of press
had turned his face brusque and pale
and slightly blue.

By the third trip up the narrow stairs, he was
winded, red and tired. That's when I offered
my woman's body, to take the heavier loads.
I carried boxes of mildewed tomes up thirty steps,
balanced on my hips, tiring too yet keeping
my breathing slow. When done, I found him
back against his truck, having another smoke.
"You put an old man to shame,"
was all he said.

I couldn't look into his face, knowing his eyes
were moist and shot with blood; I could hear
his breath heaving in his oaky chest the way
dad's did the times he tried to keep his heart
from seizing up. Instead, I bowed my head —
the way women do, the way I had some
twenty years ago when I got the final call
my dad was dead.

At last, I looked up at the man, apologized
for taking up his time; he kindly shook my hand,
then climbed into the cab of his over burdened
truck, backed down the gravel road, one arm
sticking out to leave me with his feeble
wave goodbye.

The Yoke

She seems always to be carrying
to have carried that yoke
a wood harness draping across her back
dropping buckets filled
water   seed   sod   shit
blue feathers; she masks her hard labor
with a sullen featureless face

Her body descends to bent knees
one foot lifting from the bog
the other with gold twine
linking it to the sky above

How precarious her long sunshine day
burdened yet lifted
a puzzle at field's edge
we watch her
solitary parade
rustling coins in our sad
torn pockets

After Langston

I must say yes'm to you
with the hot black coffee
burning up
the porcelain of my hand.
I must study your lead, follow
the leash of your direction
· pour tea just so. I must watch
myself . . . a green girl, vigilant
on command . . . payday comes late.
I must serve well,
hot tea for the roundtable
financiers.

Out the twentieth floor
window,
a crane batters
a nearby tower.

Country Girl

For girls who grow up dirt
poor, in the country, there are songs
the world is willing to pay
to hear. That old bucket
makes a fine rhythm drum,
the cobwebs on the barn
whistle along. Days I'd practice
low to the stacks
of hay, taking lessons
from the moon's sad loss
each month, then its hope —
growing like old hymnals.
There are always mud-soaked roads
to take once your art
is perfected. At the end of it,
a man in a slick suit
promising a gold-sequined dress
promising the stars . . .

Lesson in Ironing Handkerchiefs

The back porch picture
window floods pink
with evening.
I iron handkerchiefs,
my hand smoothing
starched linen.
I gaze into the plate glass
reflecting what I am:
a teenager bored
by her usefulness.

This is what girls used to
train on: pocket squares
to tuck against
a father's chest,
where the heart beats fastest,
where a man's hard labor
is bent and drenched
with sweat.

Occasionally I look up
from ironing, take
breath and sigh. White thread
hopes flutter past
the sycamore,
and out the back gate:
homing doves
winging a present moment
from the caught pink
of the distant past.

Grandma Shannon

Collapsed on the kitchen floor,
puddled from uremia, your own body
poisoned itself. How many times
had you rescued others yet who
was there to help you up, lift
your heavy limbs on a weightless
gurney?

At the back gate years earlier,
you never refused a meal to a hungry man
hoboing through the Depression;
straining your swollen fingers, needle-numb sore,
you supported daughters
making fine garments
for the town's best
ladies.

Your gabardine suits with such exquisite
tailoring were renown.
How did you work such perfection
into those endless seams?
You took pride in "the job worth doing
is worth doing well."

Here on the yellow kitchen counter,
your cans for coins raised
from selling vegetables,
one for tomatoes, one for beans, one
for pumpkins, making do on choked
rabbits and dust-dried fruit.

You believed in Jesus and salvation:
the way your preacher ancestors thumped
the pulpit you kneaded bread.
Grandmother, I remember you
in remnants that have been passed along
but somewhere in vague memory,
I see you standing by the plywood house,
a finger resting on your chin
like Auntie Em, calling us home.

The Drapes She Drew Back

Each morning my mother
saluted the sun,
or if no sun, the pale
refusal of light
with its winter offering.
In November she welcomed
gargantuan fog,
in March the chilled wind-curved
equinox. Each day she circled
the curtains back
away from glass
shiny and bright. Just so,
she parted my hair
to prepare me for those days
when I was ten.
With a fine-toothed comb,
she untangled the thin hair
on my head, gathered
honey-brown clumps
into two gold braids,
parted my bangs
letting light in
so that at last
I too could see out.

Bookkeeper's Daughter

There were so many years
you divided us from you,
taking the hours from the day,
subtracting them from the time
we might have learned fun,
what it is to be carefree.

Work brought home the bacon,
kept the wolf from our worn front
door; dad was never much
to help, his endless bottle
pouring down the drain.

You spent hours bent over
in your back office, accounting
lamp aglow, filling in columns,
rows of sharpened pencils
beside your coffee cup.

That world of numbers
was another father I might have
killed, the way they took you
out of reach of us:
endless sums and balance sheets,
incomes, expenses filling in
tough black ledgers, manila grids,
all those carefully penciled figures
who would never look like us.

Lesson in Record-Keeping

On the kitchen counter, grandma
kept one tin for each chicken sold,
one for tomatoes, walnuts, root
vegetables; other tins — each
with its own tight lid — savings,
coins dropped in once the visitors
went on their way back to town.

How much more could dead
rabbits bring? The ones mom
at thirteen had to kill, flops kept
in hutches outside the screened-in
kitchen door. It's hard imagining
her small hands with a quick twist,
holding the quieted affrighted beast.

Country roads are no place
for sensitive souls. Once I had
to kill a rabbit
dragged to mom's back door.
Torn open by the cat, half dead,
chuffing out blood, last breath.
It disturbed my mother so
I did the task, flattened its head
with one crush of a garden hoe.

At the bar in Overland Grill,
I bring up another small crime
against her mothering as she
balances on the stool. Old hips
ache, her feet are swollen.
Those small animals we killed
are a kind of silent pact between
us now, knowing what harm
we each can do; how many
unreconcilable thuds thunder
down those metal cans.

Lesson in Economics

She kept her wallet on the kitchen stool,
clasped by the two hands of her purse:
a Lady Buxton in prosperous days (small
sign of luxury), a worn-out vinyl billfold
from Sprouse-Reitz otherwise.

It always had a coin pocket on one side
rattling a lifetime's worth of change;
inside, a few bills tucked within a folded
leather sleeve: deep within a secret spot
she kept from everyone, including me.

I'll always have this connection: mother,
wallet, her time away at work; at home
the purse was near to hand by the kitchen
cupboards too often spilling ants.
They taunted my mother, who tried
to keep things strong and clean
along the fading shelves.

I washed dishes, cooked and dusted
house for allowances:
two dollars fifty cents that set me free
walking down Willow to shops
plunked down where olive groves,
fields of strawberries once had grown.

Or, feeling generous at the ice cream truck,
I treated neighbor kids much poorer
than we were, buying them popsicles
glistening orange, vanilla, chocolate,
dispensing my labor's own crown jewels.

Lesson in Routine

At noon, it was time for Julie's bite to eat,
a midday break in the laundry room,
where she unwrapped her long grey hair,
taking an amber comb to split it
at her crown. Then, she unslipped
tresses from her two long braids:
metallic silver threads that tumbled down.

Her lunch was a slice of toasted bread,
bologna on the side with butter;
on the stove she warmed coffee,
spooned one large scoop of sugar
into it: her midday treat. She always
stopped to pet the cat, murmuring,
then back to ironing, folding
shirts and towels, our Sunday best.

She met us when we got home from school,
fresh chocolate chips and a meat loaf
in the oven so mom could work.
What I learned from Julia was grace,
steadfastness, quiet days.

Lesson in Ethics

It was fun to shout "Boo" as Julie rounded
the kitchen corner. She had just set the iron down.
I was having a lark — age ten — lover of practical jokes.

Our elderly Dane housekeeper jumped back, gasped,
turned paler than usual — I knew what a wrong I'd done,
scaring her, wrecking the quiet of her work-day.

I had filled the serenity of her practiced labor
with a supernatural shout to erase routine:
laundering, baking, starting supper, watching us.

So she scolded me, and I knew she was right,
had taken for granted how much she did
every day while mom worked her nine-to-five.

I mistook that hard-working house as a place
for make-believe, a place for play and silliness,
where every once in a while, the women would
sit down and have a big belly laugh out loud.

Nights in White Satin

At the Rainbow, it was the one song
I danced alone, never with someone
just met. By closing and soaked
to the bone, we had danced since ten.
Out-the-door, July was dipping
below ninety and it would still be time
until the club would send us back
to our cars, our smaller valley towns.

Our stockings, shredded at the soles,
had tiny runs up the thighs; we touched them
up with pink polish. In the bathroom
at midnight, we repaired mascara
that had caked and crumbled, replaced
lipstick dulling past first bloom.

Great nights with strange partners:
the short guy with two-day stubble,
dancing with awkward abandon,
a sleeveless one who pushed hard
against my hip. The shy one we all
liked kept coming back to escort
each girl onto the dance floor.

At eighteen, nineteen, twenty, long days
at dead-end jobs, we wanted something
special for closing. Without saying why
or where I went (we would meet up
later beside locked car doors), I slipped off
to the corner of the ballroom glowing
beneath the lime-green EXIT, to sing:

"I love you, Oh, how I love you,"
to the twirling silver orb showering
colored light over the crowd — all
woozy from too much beer.
I watched the snuggled dancers;
some had known each other their

lifetimes, at least as long as the long-play
version of that Moody Blues song.

Briefly, I believed in a dreamy knight
wearing white satin out there, somewhere,
who would come and take me far
far away from that grinding town.

Libby

Every night Libby thanks the good women
who care for her: one on the weekends,
another who stays the week.

Libby repeats herself in a voice crinkled
like old yarn unraveled all day long,
frays from a yellow blanket curled
about her feet. In the dark her words
drop in a heap of silence.

From my apartment upstairs I hear
the women repeat commands in voices
that are kind yet have learned to shout
three times . . . each time up another notch:
"Do you want to urinate, urinate now,
urinate?" Then the pan that slides
across bare floor.

I hear how Libby understands, her body
stepping slowly from the bed. I have been
meaning to bring her flowers. Juanita says
she can see the red ones still. I want to say:
"I live upstairs from you," and point
to her ceiling. "Did you know that?"

One day the neighbors, Juanita, and I meet;
family members have come to remove
Libby to a rest home. We wait, our sad feelings
in uncertain heaps unraveling on Libby's
hardwood floor.

Trailer Park

Within the year when the last child had gone,
Mother sold the old house to her son
and moved to a mobile home
where the care and cleaning
was so much less a task and so we packed
her goods into boxes, wrapped
the crystal glasses, porcelain plates,
and helped her make the move.

We planted a magnolia, and roses:
two rows in the hard-packed soil.
On mornings I visited, we took our coffee
and the sunrise on the small back step
looking east in our slippers and gowns.
She held her cigarette and I my juice
as we looked through the ivy that graced
the trailer's metal frame, to an empty field:
clods and stickers, nettles, burrs, and the
occasional flitter of a red-winged blackbird.

It was her way to pray she said, leaning
against the railing, inhaling silver smoke
in the misty air as we both stared out
across the rough brown field.
Her housedress was a simple pale blue,
a pocket for her Kleenex and Pall Malls,
a lighter she worked enough to keep her hands
from the chill. Her hazel eyes, tired
from fifty years of labor, and yes, from
raising us, grew moist when we caught
a glimpse of darting hares: angels dancing
along the horizon of a simpler place.

Mail-Order Bride

While she folds their sheets
        he stands
accusing her, has she been
        snitching quarters?
A blur of blue towels flumps
        in the dryer;
his underwear spins. He towers
        over his small
imported brown-skin wife.

Lumbering back to the bench
        he watches her
folding clothes, hanging shirts.
        She drops
another quarter in, bustles
        under eyes that hold
her like an unseen rope.
        She slows,
lowers her gaze to a basket
        piling high.

I see him talking with Mr. Wino
        who just arrived,
asking for spare change, a dime
        for coffee; the two men
share smokes and chat; I see
        the wife relax.
She talks with their teenage daughter;
        the women laugh soft
but nervously, when across the room
        the man's voice booms:
"Roll the socks, damn it, don't tie them
        into knots."

The daughter's breath is caught;
        I hear her whisper
a faint, "o.k., I didn't know."
        Together

the two young women roll
      his socks,
pitch them in the laundry cart:
      blue and dark-brown balls
getting stuck in the wires
      of the laundry cart:
they look at one another, then at me
      and smile.

Maids

Each day, I go up with the maids,
come down in the evening alone.

Each day the bus rolls to the curb.
I climb up the hill, newspaper in hand.

The maids are already on the bus.
They have come from further off.

They rose earlier to go to houses
where professors and scientists live.

To clean bedrooms, hallways, parlors
they go up to the grand hotel.

The Claremont Hotel, like a white
Falcon, looming on top of the hill.

The fault-line runs under ground.
It is where the incline begins.

Guests forget about fault-lines, play
on the tennis courts, in pools.

Every day, I ride to my secretarial job
with the brown maids in simpler clothes.

We ride up the hill, to offices and rooms.
but, I never see them come down.

Our faces bedraggle with sleep, not one
of us ready to face crumpled sheets,

Stacks of papers, files to sort out.
There are melted cocktail cubes

running across marble countertops,
bathrooms with tear-stained sinks.

With the maids I go up every morning
We chat and we chat, then wave goodbye.
Goodbye to the driver who kindly
Lets us out, sets us down on the street —

He has many more maids to deliver,
more maids than one can picture.

Her Boss

Scratches at his crotch
when giving dictation.
She notices this, a small tic
at the edge of her eye,
continues transcription.
Formalities of correspondence
keep mixing her up.
There he goes again,
leaning back on his swivel
chair, stuffed full, belly
slipping past his belt.
He grabs himself, motions
with a wave of his
opposite hand; she should
proceed jotting words down,
missives to an unjust world.
She writes it all down,
every urgent syllable.
In the July heat, sweat
beads on his brow. Still,
she labors on quietly
beneath half-held breath.
Just out of school, she had
thought she was ready
for the world, was ready
to make a difference. Now,
she wonders why they never
taught her to transcribe
certain gestures into words.

Girl Friday

When greeted by her husband's girl, she smiles
not wide with teeth, but tight and white.

Tennis togs and sculpted hair, a perspiration glow,
missus bounces in: might hubby be around? But, no.

He's out. She regales the office girl with news:
her investment club, a trip to sunny Spain.

Enthused about robotics, the processing of oil,
she pauses, checks her watch, solicits praise.

The office she designed, isn't it a lovely shade
of oatmeal tan? Then, there is the paneling,

Latticework and a Japanese showcase fan.
She was thinking "something calm and plain,

Accented by drapes of tinted rose, antique stain."
The hand-placed vases stuffed with dried flowers,

Hand-picked straw ones, so exquisitely arranged,
yet. . . bold. "It really is a marvelous change?"

Telephone rings, the younger woman answers
while the boss's wife surveys the room *and* her:

Couldn't she spend some money, buy some hose?
Get shoes that aren't so plain and tailored clothes?

It's time to move along she thinks; their eyes meet:
"ta ta" the boss' wife sing-songs, slips out to tea.

Finally, office to herself, Girl Friday can relax;
behind the fine oak desk, she considers her next task.

Unpolished nails thrum the handle of the phone;
she dials, waits, then hums a snippet of a song.

Some Woody Guthrie tune, I think, with rhyme:
"this train's bound for glory" one more time.

100 California Street

She brought me to the fine cherry-wood
cabinet and unlocked the first door.
Each cup and saucer were perfect bone China,
delicate, gold-lipped. Each worth over
two-hundred dollars, she warned
as we placed a set of twelve on two
ivory-inlaid trays to carry them
into the boardroom where later,
financiers would wrangle over budgets,
futures, venture-capital projects,
whose dreams they might fund.

She showed me how to brew the perfect
pot of tea, how to set the silver stirring
spoons astride each saucer, how to polish
the silver service. I was just a temporary
girl, but the English secretary
would train me still, as though an afternoon
might become a lifetime. After we set
each linen napkin down, she looked
around the large blank room, while I
stared out the clear picture window
toward any bridge that might take me
out of there.

Secretary's Lament

How tight the mower man
must make his corners, retracing
steps he made just last month.
Tufts missed, he pauses to wonder at.
The green in the stone-cast shade
is a perfect parallelogram.
He thinks how all lives parallel
the world where he works,
astride his mechanical lawn groomer.
Here a pocket for fresh flowers
but he must remove last week's
offering. And, how glorious a day,
sun over Mountain View, rolling green
hills, acacias starting to turn
from canary yellow, smell of a baby's bottom,
to the mustardy of May.
Palms, non-fruiting plums, and pine.
I envy the groundskeep
his full day out of doors; for me,
the rest here
in the cemetery is only enough time
for a bag lunch and brisk walk.
So, like him, I start the engine,
he, his mower, me my mother's Saturn,
and, I think of her gone to ground
as I return to my own cubicle,
an office where I stack white papers,
trim files, close out dead accounts.

Catch that Train, I'm Leaving

Hi, I'm Julie. I'm here
to help you make your reservation.
We offer two destinations
to your afterlife: please speak
your selection loudly and clearly.
Do you want the train
for Heaven or for Hell?

I'm sorry I didn't understand your answer.

Ok. I got it. Let me check availability
and we can make your reservation in just
a moment.
Tick tick tick click click click tic tic

Ok. I'm back. I'm sorry but accommodations
for train travel to Heaven
are booked for the next few years.
We could reroute you through Limbo.
Would you like to see if that is available?

I'm sorry. Was that a yes? I wasn't sure.

O.k. I've got it. Let me check availability.
Shall I proceed? That's great. Tick tick tick
click click click tic tic . . . Hi, I'm back.

You are now booked on a one-way train,
departing 2:45 p.m. on Sunday.
There is no check-in for luggage. Please
do not bring any liquids or combustibles,
in your carry-on luggage. And, keep
your baggage with you at all times.

We know you have many choices in
your travel arrangements and thank you
for choosing us.

Out of the Box

When young, I didn't know about the ceiling
made of glass, nor about those workplace rules
that over time would leave me kneeling.

I bought that line about hard work, plain-dealing,
thought I'd succeed by acquiring the right tools.
When young, I didn't know about the ceiling.

Bumping my head against it sent me reeling.
Encounters with some bosses were more like duels;
over time the battles left me kneeling.

The only way to stave off unpleasant feeling
was to tell myself I didn't want those frills.
When young, I didn't know about the ceiling,

although I'd watched mom's years of peeling
thickened layers of paint, cow-towing to old fools.
Over time, it left my mother kneeling,

exhausted, bitter and unaware she needed healing.
Well, damn, I'm worth more than store-bought jewels.
When young, I didn't know about the ceiling:
how, over time, it could leave one kneeling.

Drugstore Girl

From behind the other counter, the druggist
surveyed the way she rang up candy for neighbor kids,
tobacco for the priest from Saint Thérèse,
sodas for the hippie in his yellow cotton batik.

Clerking her way through college, she'd been
promised a raise and stood vigilant behind
the humidor, kept her cash tidy in the drawer.
Innocent as placebo, she was pale and thin,
loved the valley's hot dry breeze against
fresh-shaved shins. Summer days, she watched
front glass doors swing open, closed, and open
yet again. She waited on retirees and kids
who carried notes, ladies after playing golf
needing hair dye, cigarettes, a quart of gin.

She studied the nervous tics of elder dames
who crossed linoleum half-blind behind their canes
to stop at the Hallmark bin. They seemed to spend
all day lifting cards up toward the ceiling,
decoding secrets scratched under condolences.

Then, there was Bill, her boss, dark hair
oiled like Joe Friday's who praised her handwriting
but scrutinized the way she waited on
"his customers." The day the young black man
came in, Chuck's breath caressed her neck
as he leaned in behind stogies and the case
of Plexiglass® where Timex watches swirled.

And, didn't she hear his urgent whisper?
"Gotta keep your eye out for that kind."
On her shoulder, his hand, as she thrummed
white slips he passed, prescriptions signed
by doctors that were so very hard to read.
Assigned to the task, she did what she was told,
one eye on the druggist, the other trained
on the customer, watching for the crime
one of them was bound to commit.

Rebel, Rebel

When the seventies sizzled on
in cities north and south, in Fresno
we didn't know why those fires burned —
we worked swingshifts. Kids dropped down
after two-job days before heading home
and getting stoned. Nowhere else to go,
except the drag, so they came to us.
Every Saturday night we cued up hits,
and records spun hot and fast
beneath fluorescent tubes —
our only rebel flares.

Those working lights were like the lie-
detector tests we had to take to get
those stupid jobs. I once met a man
at Motel 6 on Blackstone Ave. who strapped
rubber-coated wires across my chest,
then asked: *what drugs I took?*, tried to get me
to confess was I *straight or gay?* (Who knows
why it made a diff just to have some clerk
take his cash?) Maybe it kept some honest
or more scared; later we just joked,
there's a reason why they call them *chains*.

Around midnight when we had to close,
I vacuumed endless slips of cellophane,
candy crushed into the rug the teeny-boppers
dropped who'd gotten bored with Bob's Big Boy
and came to us until we locked them out.
Then, don't you know, we cranked it up:
 "Gloria" by Patti Smith or "Money" by the Floyd,
Bowie's "Rebel Rebel," other tunes
that turned it upside down for us
working kids at last.

Greetings from the Vogue Accessory Editor
(A found poem taken from the "Today Show," March 1990)

We believe in the scarf
We believe in the sling-back shoe

People should wear gloves
It's a nice pulled-together look

This is a nice new *Vogue* look

We love pearls
And the cuff
The double-cuff
What suits your mood, there are no rules

This is a nighttime look
I don't think you'd be going
      to the office wearing this

What you need for Spring:
sling-back shoe, set of good pearls,
definitely, a good pastel
      hand bag, peach or lemon,
whatever suits you.

Traffic Jam With Pantyhose by the Wayside

Who were these women who threw
caution to the concrete edges,
dropped pantyhose from long windows
of sports cars, sedans, sleek black Mariah's?
Who were they: these dames in saffron
or fuchsia colored underthings,
lacewing styles, designer tights?
Someone dropped her sensual leg-wraps overboard
where the freeway curves around the city,
toward the bridge.

Here billboards blare and traffic cramps
in Indian summer heat. Here my worn legs
press home along with all the others.

Every Night She Swallows the Sun

After a visit to the San Jose Rosicrucian Museum.

It is not on her way to work,
commuter traffic piled up
at the toll booth, her hair
already losing its hold.
And it is not when the notes
stacked on her desk rise higher
than pharaoh's obelisk.
It is not even after a long day
when she inscribes
what must be carried forward
to the next day's list.

It is after evening she performs
the task, the ritual: in the throes
of lovemaking, when he bends
to kiss the feathered parting
of her thighs, and the bed turns
into an orange-red chant, and her back
arches against the indigo linen
canopy of night. Then, her alabaster
hips thrust against the dark.

Only then does she do it, swallow
the sun, lifting instead
the sloe-eyed moon above
moist and hearty hips.
In one deep swallow,
gulp of fiery wholeness
she satisfies herself
for yet another day.

Earthquake, Taiwan, 1999

Like me women stunned by grey walls
suddenly folding in; they climb
from their beds now strewn madly
with splinters, glass, plaster chips
as wide as broken hands.

They wonder as I do: has life caved in?
Surely not a stone building with such
promise of prosperity? Surely not the city
with its glaze of neon signs telling us
that we are on our way to the future?

They stumble in smoke corridors,
spot a lantern's passing flash,
scrape along the fallen floor
with bloody knees; then one phone
gets a signal, seems to work.

Can you see me? Can you save me?
The snuffling of rescue dogs
know release is close as the settling wall,
the elevator stuck in its desperate shaft,
the next heavy floor that dropped
endlessly upon them.

Public Servants & Professionals

Urban Knight

"Don't move. Be still. Stop. STOP!"
The wheelchair motor revs again.
Passengers wait and watch
our driver in his large black gloves.
"I won't do this if you keep moving."
A hook dangles behind the wheelchair
of an old deaf Chinese man: confused,
he clasps the small throttle on his arm-rest,
stopping then starting his chair.

"Don't move. Stop. Stop. STOP!"
It's a full bus: heading downtown
to work, to shop, to check in with
a parole officer, collect a welfare check,
pay the water bill, provide a birth
certificate, see a man about a job.
"Does anyone speak his language?"
The driver removes one glove, lifts
his light brown palm: red flag before
a stubborn bull. He catches the strap
over the hook, laces the seat belt
across the rider's back. The bus rolls
forward again and picks up speed,
the wheelchair man safely secured.
Stop, start, stop. Doors open, close.
No one reported the patient, kind,
able driver who got us to our final
destinations: this is the only record.

Late Arrival

The metallic skin train ripples
into Civic Center station.
Down the escalator, she races:
doors of the subway train
opening and closing — rubber pads
clicking dully as she reaches
its final closing thuds. Twenty minutes
'til the next train: "damn,"
she says softly. No one notices
her private agony; they have all felt it.
The station underground:
electronic, metallic, rubber, all
softness is in the empty surrounding
space, a hollow tube up the city's gut.
Suddenly, the doors open again,
just for her, the late-arrival.
A faceless driver at the front —
knight with a red cape flung
across the puddle,
offering his hand.

Traffic Dancer

Some men love to direct traffic. You can tell
by the stars on their chests and the way
their fingers point in the direction of free motion.

I love to watch these traffic dancers with their
blue jackets and sunburned hands. I love to
weave through their patterns honking my horn.

Always stuck in this intersection like
a Taoist wheel, central to the hub,
these saints of the road.

Typhoon

The peasant leads the journalist through the lowlands
where Burma raises its daily rice, where the typhoon
struck hardest, knocking animals, houses, tools,
everyone down.

Halfway across the globe, I sit in my soft bed, cat curled
between my thighs. It is not helplessness I feel:
I am bone tired.

My working hands swollen from a week of typing;
my tea chills after forgetfulness; my television flashes
devastating news.

Burma's lowlands are green-grey. The peasant speaks
his foreign tongue; the translator tries translating anguish
to the reporter.

And around the world, the audience tries to understand
how the stench of bloated bodies
sickens them.

Through a Medium

Eyes meet eyes, touch, contact across time,
the timelessness about which we know
nothing at all.

How studious to count these stories
as important.

Documentation is the fine line around boxes
of text, of something said
in the flat grains of photographic paper.

Skin cells burned into film,
brought back to life.

Take for example, this mill boy:
posed, elbow bent, fist in mouth.
Raw hurt in his eyes, far older
than his eight or nine years.
Tattered shirt, torn coveralls.
The cap adrift in lint.

Or, these colliers: faces blackened,
standing before their black pits.
Five pairs of coal-dust rubbed eyes.
An exhaustion that knows no end
at the dark of the work heavy day.

Or, finally, the testimony of the camera
to the decaying bodies found
at Auschwitz or Dachau, the
prisoners of Buchenwald
pointing out their tattoos.

Eyes all downcast in shallow graves of eyes.
Our own eyes becoming momentarily
locked into theirs.

Over the Rainbow

Some days all you can do is avoid spilling
coffee, rushing off to work, briefcase
under your arm, paper cup in hand.

You begin by juggling parcels, packages
while you lean into the warehouse door
to turn the key, triggering the alarm.

The cup tips, you loosen your grip; spilling
coffee you scald your hand. Still, you can
squeeze in through the employee door.

You hasten to silence the alarm you've set off.
How much better to catch your breath
and settle in.

All day, you watch hordes of Canada geese
across the road. Those filthy migrant
birds stomping down the silver dew.

High over their unfluttered dusky wings,
clouds appear, looking like parachutes
dropped in a foreign war.

All day, you hear "boom boom boom."
The ballpark keeper's loudspeaker attempts
to scare away the birds.

I sit at my desk, stare out at the unflustered
geese, rub salve on my burns; all I can think about
is my country's limitless thirst for war.

The Audit

I'm an honest person, forgive me. In accounting
school, I came close to flunking a final for which
I had not studied rather than cheat off someone else.

I've always taught my children that story
about the father of our country, how he chopped
the cherry tree and could not tell a lie.

I used to preach "honesty is the best policy."
But this time, something changed; I wanted
to get away with it. When the final bill arrived,

I caught the miscalculation, one-hundred dollars
in our favor, and I let it slide. (With what we pay
that guy I know he can still feed his family).

Didn't Franklin claim, "A penny saved is a penny
that you've earned"? At grocery stores, I'm the guy
who goes back to the clerk when given wrong change.

Someone ends up paying for such mistakes (a teller
charged against her wage, a bookkeeper fired).
But when that bill landed on my desk, I paid it.

I paid just what it said, even before it was due —
then tucked the statement into the file. I sure did please
the boss who has promised me a raise.

He tells me: "Don't sweat it, it's just your job
to write the checks," then laughs at any doubt,
glad I've finally learned to do things his way.

Consensus Group

Seventeen citizens gather at the Hyatt Regency in a windowless
conference room with their laundry list to set before the State to
explore if there is harm caused by electro-magnetic fields from
power lines overhead. And we sit for hours, conferencing under
brittle fluorescent light bearing down, an overhead projector flashing
frizzled grey light on diagrams and charts, a silver urn sputtering
more coffee all day above its burner. We're all spending energy in
this stale room empty of agreement between scientists and doctors,
departments of health and departments of energy and utility execs,
the voluntarily sincere and citizens concerned. Words spin
like molecules, frizzled encoded suspicions built on mutual distrust.
We consult and find the limits of our consensus, drink more soda,
coffee, tea, while somewhere in California, those power lines keep
pumping out endless transmissions and the wind turbines cut down
another solitary falcon in the dust.

Co. Rep's Rd. Trip*

In big hotels these days keys are cards.
You insert the card the key into your door:
a green light signals if you're lucky, opens
if you're lucky. You enter the starched room,
throw your suitcase down on a bed big
as Manhattan, set the alarm to ensure
you'll arrive on time. There are lights
to switch on turn down, and your neighbor's
TV blasts. (You want to punch the wall.)

Turn on the radio, scroll oldies, classics, jazz —
whatever you need, strip off jacket and belt,
the hose with a run, till you're down to your slip.
You toss on casual wear, head for the bar,
a nightcap or two but on your return
(between lounge and your room), your key,
the plastic card with magnetic strip
has been lost so you wait and you wait
till the concierge shows up and then tip,
feel grateful, give thanks. You're exhausted,
and know you need sleep, But, you're restless:

room service shut down an hour ago. Well,
you do what you can: make notes, check messages,
place an expensive call. Hear the elevator
drop down its well, shake the feeling and thumb
the remote: late night talk with a freshly shaved host.
You can just about smell the lotion he wears, admire
the cut of the tie at his throat, his wavy dark hair.

The room temperature really dries out your eyes —
you think: draw a bath. Over the faucet's cascade,
another sound arrives: a sad melody like a dream
that's been lost. In the next door room, a violin plays.
You step in the tub — just a quick soak — and realize
at once, it's all the warmth you can stand.

* corporate jargon for company representative's road trip

Familiar

The black bear bounds out of the elevator
before I do, before I can
explain. It's too late, security's been called.
Smurfy sniffs the air: coffee. Heads toward
the employee lounge where a big pink box
of doughnuts sits barely touched.
He eats a crüller, a double-frosted, maple
chocolate-cake not thinking about diet,
cholesterol, trans-fats, hydrogenation:
for this, I love him. He lifts off his haunch
to full height, a pastry in each paw,
leads me to my oatmeal-tan cubicle
where my screen saver flashes his picture.
I smile at his approving wild warm eyes
when, pop, zing, Hussein, the guard delivers
dart drugs from his gun. "Hussein!"
I holler, "He's my guest for this week's
'bring your familiar to work day'!"
Too late, my Smurf is down, and I crawl
to the floor beside his bulky head,
waving a vial of honey to revive
the gentle giant, the one who keeps
this office job completely real.

BFD at the BOA*

Downtown Berkeley, October 27, 2008

Under the raging geyser, white water spiking
above the sidewalk — we have an unexpected
Old Faithful — when two angel fish in yellow
slickers dive toward the spigot. The crowd
gathers in the pink city dusk: onlookers who
press noses against an invisible aquarium
of air to watch Berkeley's firemen battle
the heaving upward blast. One man passes
a wrench-like tool — some kind of tourniquet
(since we do not know its name) — to his partner.
The traffic stills: streetlights blink red; the cops
have halted all routine. Patiently, the pair circle
the hydrant, twisting their wrench: they seem
like odd-shaped dolphins swimming out to ride
Poseidon down, while we stand in our peanut
gallery, cynical Berkeley mouths flabbergasted
until water plummets to the ground. Then, all
smiles erupt. The wrestled cyclone has thrilled
the citizenry but the men simply don their coats
from the BFD, turn shyly toward the red truck.
Thundering applause and riotous laughs erupt.
The hydrant chokes some final drops, the police
re-open routes. Evening settles in, the People's
Republic makes its way home, our faith in public
servants safely strangely patriotically renewed.

* *Berkeley Fire Department; Bank of America*

Prayer for the Workers

At five past eight they pour coffee, greet coworkers
                              walk down long halls,
eat morning buns, bagels, *pan dulce*,
                              make hasty calls.
By eight-thirty the caffeine has finally kicked in,
                              a man tunes
a small radio he keeps below his desk where boss
                              can't see.
Others pause, remembering last night's argument,
                              an exceptional meal,
the outstanding double-play, amazing steal.

There are plans to arrange, calls to return, appointments
                              to be made,
then there's that insecure salesman, a decision
                              to delay.
A secretary places her catalog order before too late,
                              pink chenille bedspread
she can finally afford, now on sale, then time to
                              buckle down,
get out that report. No one knows what's coming, the plane
                              on its way, the one
that has just hit; a few dig for cell phones in large purses
                              quick call to home
tell the kids that they're o.k., then wait instruction, for someone
                              to tell them what to do.
Faces press against plate glass for any clue. By nine a.m., some
                              return to their desks,
take pictures down and hold them to their chests
                              while impatience builds.
Finally, a few take the lead and stairwells fill with workers
                              (like me)
trying to get out, desperate for breath.
                              I imagined this.
Every job is a kind of theft. There are scars
                              in the lives we lead;
I can only pray
                              for words to honor those who die
at work: three-thousand strong yet gone
                              without a trace.

A Book Clerk Considers the Winds of Change

I work in a bookstore.
I witness rows of books
on topics that expand and contract.
Right now, the shelves on Iraq,
Afghanistan, Iran fill like goats.
I must adjust the width
for history. From Taliban
to the Shia revival, space opens and fills,
titles descend from publishers,
right and left points of view,
perpetually arguing, point-counter-
pointing their fears and causes.
For awhile the shelf on Afghanistan
shrunk while the ones about Iraq
more than doubled.

This is a warning to all you countries,
all you ancient worlds:
don't let writers come
to interview you. Stay quiet, tucked
inside your regions.
When opinions and reflections
start up on Charlie Rose, CNN,
Fox News, Meet the Press, the borders
of our bookshelves stretch and bow:
that's how you'll know America is
on its way to discovering you.

Motivational Speaker

Hugs his microphone, wears Dockers, has a boat.
My, how he Frisbees out
words with a grin.

Someday soon . . . following his advice, I too
will see my ship come in
will have a life of brilliant ease
upon the gravy train; will find
my ace in the hole.

Some Landlords

Not much has changed since the enclosures
and the clearances, the markets
über all, even the squeaky minds
of some landlords.
When not burning thatched rooftops,
prefects standing guard, they are shaming
the way their tenants live. Once,
a landlord waltzed in to show off
the paint job I had done when I was
bathing: no doorbell ring or knock,
just a 'how do you do.' One replaced
metal wires with plastic ones, then sent
her goon on Christmas Eve, eviction
papers in her hand. I am not the down-
troddenest, poorest poor slob who walks
these bayside streets, just a person working
hard to pay unseasonable rents.
And what of those most truly poor?
Well, they crowd the rooms with families
of twelve or ten and make do. And we
are not supposed to squeak or squawk,
or tell our friends, just take the key,
close the door, relieved to have a tent.

Stock Market

That one has a limp; this one bolts
in cold weather; others are
only skin, bare bruised bone,
skeletally unsound, at a loss
when sold for starch or glue,
food for hounds.

For many, the banks struck up
dirty loans,
put debtors under water
in deep regret
even before the ink had dried,
the borrowers returned "home."

As it all crashed down,
the bitter stink
alerted us to tarnished chrome,
the plastic paint
under seeming chariots of gold.

Still, no rebuke: our system
made complicit every one
who crowded into stands
around the track. Some fell
short, could not see
the fun; looking overhead,
they saw the ceiling crack.
Could sniff the frightened horses,
hear the gun.

"Home Sales Rise"
San Francisco Chronicle, Friday, April 20, 2012

There's nothing quite like the point we hit bottom.
Only prices can start to rise. Some sellers unaware
of buyers, the bank'll short-sell homes, eat loss
like breakfast cereal on the oak-wood tables they use
to stage the illusion, a trick to make the world of home
seem warm and stable. I tell everyone houses come,
houses go. Jump in when the roller coaster hits
its lowest, homes have just emptied out, families
evicted; that's when the timing's right, you can make
your biggest buck. The data are all still choppy,
the robo-signing scandal put the El Caibosh
on foreclosures, sent some reeling. Tight inventory
is today's realtor reality, prices so fragile families
are on the street. We mustn't worry; they'll pull
through. Don't guilt-trip me. Underwater.
Shit, they just didn't get aboard the raft
when they should've. It's no one's fault the banks
closed in, smelling something like sweat and blood
equity in the fall-out of the American dream.

It's All About the Numbers

They stand in a long line, blocking
the aisle at our local Safeway,
clutching one, ten, twenty dollar bills,
waiting for their numbers
to come up. It's the biggest
lottery on record, and even though
there's a greater likelihood
of getting hit by a bolt of lightning,
they are patient to queue, then
punch their numbers, let the die
roll where it may. I suppose all
humankind will always have this
glimmer of hope, that if it places
itself in the right spot at the right
time, as at the place where the
rainbow sets its old weary body down,
a pot of gold will spill on its shoulder.
What they always forget is that
when the skies open, the brazen
metal shoots out, it could be
a cracking blow, something that
erases everything and turns the brain
into mush, forever shifting that
portion of hope into some deranged
element of shocked despair.

Blue *Reboso*

I am tired of my tailored shirts
and long to sit all day
under the oak in a long blue *reboso*.

A long blue *reboso* drapes
my shoulders and lets the sky enter
where my shoulder blades clip like wings.

Blades have clipped my wings:
blades that are sharp like America
where we never wear *rebosos*.

In America we wear big red ties
and tell stories as *gordo*
as the Rio Grande after summer storms.

After storms we put on our big red ties,
go to the big *Mercado*,
where cash registers clink.

The sound of cash registers clinking
overshadows the soft *guitarra*. Too much
competition, music lost in haste.

In the haste, I lose touch with myself,
mad as a gnat in my crisp tailored shirt,
my red *gordo* tie; I've forgetting the oak.

Forgetting the oak, we lose touch —
our hearts become sandy river beds.
The only blue to be seen:
an abandoned *reboso*.

La Llorona

(The Weeping Woman)

In the darkened room, Mr. Lopez
places his final touch on a small crib,
the pine box, lacquered and layered
with padded white satin.
When the procession reaches
the coffin maker,
the men lift the filled cradle
of the child's death and for an endless hour
carry it out of town
into the tan desert, lower it —
so white and clean —
into hard pan soil
bereft from drought.
There *la llorana* watches them
from her *arroyo seco*; she leans
toward the women and weeps,
pulled by the tide of her own sorrow,
and listening to the streaming plaints
of those who must bury and bury
the bread of their births. Given life,
then denied the gift, as if
it comforted her own grief.
All eyes turn to *azul* skies where
Holy Ones rain down. Above,
children hover
in magellanic clouds
as women inter love to this dust soil,
accepting their blessed
with open mouths, sending
what is needed to ripen their tongues
with *pan dulce* tears.

Mortician's After Hours

He undresses her at night, after the final
viewing when the family has abandoned
her vibrant body to the cold shelf
of death. He pinches the zipper, plunges it
down her spine; with breathy tugs, he pulls
at shoulders, unfolds the sleeves, turns
the dress back into its root sack. Her golden
face changes under vague fluorescent light,
the ingénue gleam becomes the sticky
whore of death. He listens carefully
for cheek bones rattling his ear. At home
there is no wife, a pantry incomplete
with jam jars, butter cookie tins, freezer
long since frozen shut. What he does
in the dark, no one could excuse or love:
her stockings useless now. He kisses lips
that do him in. He kisses cheeks, he takes
his hand to her eternity to please himself.
The ritual is brief and silent, yet calms
his early morning dream. And afterwards,
he muses on his artist role, begins to see
his life just as it is, remembers vaguely
a wife he lost, and one-time friends.
At a recent noon he felt the warm press,
the sister's hand which gave him a sense
of normalcy: even a solitary man can need
this at times. Later, climbing up the subway
stair into frost-bite wind, he will finger
kind words in his pocket, words to share
with ones so far; he carries them all day
yet never finds a mailbox to send these
scribbled messages along their way.

Express Market

In its weighty *sans serif* font, **Express Market**
should have lasted forever. The brown awning —
sturdy enough — the street corner among the busiest.

Its windows are now doused in dark paint
letting neighbors know not to come in
for bread, eggs, another quart of milk.

It's been a long time since flour bags were raised,
then stacked along the grocer's shelves, since
peaches and grapes were displayed in silver bins.

Typefaces can lie; some fonts project solidity
where none exists. Bold letters mask weakness,
scripts promise pleasures routinely denied.

At night, when the world has turned indoors,
some wait at bus stops, others traipse diagonally
across the road, hands gripped on plastic bags.

Express Market is code for men who gather
after hours to crouch on soiled linoleum, toss
their yellowed bones, a druggy drop-off.

Perhaps a place for criminal cabals. No light
leaks in, no sound slips under doors to let
the neighborhood know there's hope in store.

STARBUCKS

I had tromped around San Miguel all day in my new *huaraches*,
delighted by colorful hand-painted signs, my new vocabulary:
botanícas, dulces, joyería. Fine filigreed lettering with droplets
of ampersands, exclamation marks in hand-painted amethyst,
turquoise, jade, and the wide rainbow of native opal.

But turning at the northwest corner of the plaza, I faced
American enterprise refusing to reside in the background.
You can tell by its *sans serif* demi-bold signage: heavy
letters splayed across the quiet grey of Mexican stone.

We *Americanos* need to be seen. Louder, brighter, bolder,
wearing shorty-shorts in *las iglesias*, chartreuse halter tops
en el járdin. Even the ex-pats' sullen expressions reek
from superiority; faces baked into sun-drawn skin
watch curious *touristas*. I wonder, though:

What did they leave behind when they packed block type,
Arial Bold in their overstuffed *equipajes?* When they
squatted in a foreign land to "live like kings"
with hired maids, gardeners, cooks, others to do their work
so they can look down on us fresh-eyed lovers
of exotic type?

Grace Beauty Supply

The bus skids past the seedy shop
where *Grace Beauty Supply* luxuriates
above the second floor. On the marquee,
stretched in odalisque italic font,
light blue letters nestle against
a background of cotton candy pink.

One might think of Marie Antoinette,
Mae West, or Gwen Stefani, the full
shape of female form: the mistresses
French painters fantasized about
as they dabbed pink at the nipple,
deep brown in the darkest culverts.

My imagination carries me too far
as I roll down San Pablo Avenue
(number seven-two) after a working day.
At *Grace Beauty Supply*, posters
peel back from their corners,
headshots featuring recent styles
bleach into greying blue from hot
west-facing suns.

That's how women appear walking
the street below. Black women tempted
by a sale of wigs-gone-blonde,
white women with Mata Hari bobs,
girls with colored strips and dreads,
ringlets, tattoos, piercings: we can be
anything with Gracie's touch.

East Bay Rats

Some of these desperate shacks
should have collapsed by now.
The bus speeds past storefronts,
shaking us down over potholes,
every bump. I try seeing Oakland
block by block, need to change
how I look at this wretched town.

Poor seedy San Pablo. This game
I play to pass time: separating old
from new on a barely reconstructed
drover's road. Yesterday, police
circled another crime scene at
the Pump 'n Go. A panicked woman
jumped onto the bus: *"Oh boy, Oh man,*
what they catching now?"
A strange man grunted:
"Uh, umh. Same old, same old."

On the other side was a sign:
East Bay Rats Motorcycle Club
hand-painted black in Gothic type
above two bright red doors.
I imagined large gruff men
gathering there to roll the die,
winning a lasting camaraderie.

Anyone who makes the world
a better place unto themselves,
and signals to their friends
in Blackletter font, **We Are The East Bay Rats** . . .
well, they're just like me, trying
to make some fun in a world
that spends way too much
of its time in a living Helvetica.

Police Training Unit

It begins — this career — with names
emblazoned across the back:
Campanella, Tyree, Lee, Zondervan, Price, McDevitt, Sukosky.

Walking the Oakland street, half a block away,
I notice the simple font inscribing each
uniformed officer.
Butler, DeJesus, Frankenheimer, Wong.

Yet, each man is a shade apart from his comrade;
skin tones range from mahogany to pinky-beige,
from sallow to ruddy rough to pale.

The recruits will swear to keep the peace,
maintain society's tenuous hold, will risk
their lives day after day.
Johnson, Deschutes, Rincon, MacDonald, Olson.

For now, they gather on an abandoned frontage
for a lesson about asphalt, skidding to stops,
not noticing the woman walking by.

I contemplate each blue name written in a standard
yet decorative font, chuckling that it isn't
"Copperplate," "Impact," or "Kung Fu Gothic."

Years of setting type made me see how letters
are like people: some formal, others flaky,
some foreign, some native, until
Singh, Martin, Armstrong, Grier, Marcovicci.

Men to uphold, protect the law, I may
need to call someday when name
and font won't matter.

Du Fu, Li Po, and Dr. Everwine

Dr. Everwine sat on his desk and hunched
toward our small class,
a cigarette and its breathy smoke
snaking to the window, half opened.

Only twenty yet suddenly,
I saw through an old man's eyes:
the professor, grey-haired and subtle,
quietly reading Du Fu and Li Po.

Ancient Chinese poets
in long white beards sounding
the ten-thousand chimes
of their losses.

Drunken poets dancing beside a river
as far from Fresno as we could imagine.

And they laughed intimately
as if they knew
we first-time students
of ancient Chinese poets
were about
to fall in.

Auto Commute Death of Teacher Who Maintained Second Job Site at Home

He was just
going to and from
work and home
with a front seat
splashed
with papers
to correct
and a grade book
when the lights
changed, he didn't see what
ran the red, hit
him broadside; just saw
the space
around him flutter
first and final
drafts
white speckled birds
shocked
by electric wire.

All testimony
witnessing the fact
made the point
that the teacher took work home,
saved hours at school
for student raps,
studies of paragraphs
and parsings,
and the occasional lapse
into how
metaphor
can weave magic.

Still the court
refused to grant
his widow workers' comp:
questioning his
place of work or home.

They determined
the teacher was off duty
in his auto commute between
the two locales.

Some migrations
are best in their
transitions: the soul, for instance,
who takes flight
above the open air
where an ambulance whirr
screams above the line
on roads
that judgment
tends to blur.

Teacher, Retired

The retired teacher next door has cataracts,
can barely hear; all day, her television roars
down the narrow alley between her kitchen
and mine, where the vines overgrow:
orange lantana, blue-green wandering Jew,
where an oak comes within an inch
of losing its own slow life to urban blight.
From my office window I can see her living
room through a collection of blue bottles
that gather dust along her sill. At night,
she shuffles through white-stained doors.

One day I'll look across, glimpse her body
collapsed on the carpet; wonder if she is dead.
I won't have a number to call; such times
we live in when we know our neighbors
so intimately and not at all, when I —
a poor teacher myself — stares at the future,
knowing how history repeats itself in blue
bottles, lonely houses, spooky rooms.

Social Worker's Lamentation

So many I tried to help and failed,
I could smell desperation
like when farmers burn decaying leaves:
the scent hangs low, caught
in the valley between the peaks of mountains.

Caught in the tines, the pitchfork
lives tossed toward flame.
I watched, filed the right reports,
met deadlines, enrolled a few in plans
(the ones who the state contends
have qualified); there is little
help, really, as misery compounds.

This is a society on a declining path;
the monied fear the weakest ones,
reward wealth managers instead.

I'm a kind of accountant, tracking
the progress or regress of souls.

So, whether it is the house burnt down
or closed accounts, I may become
a change agent for this
irreparable helplessness.

My own suffering,
my own constant
emptiness turns grey
with late harvest smoke.

Words Under Fingertips

Words pour under his fingertips: rainy, cloudy,
dark, all kinds of weather. He does not
make the connection between the picture of ice
on the trees, a black cloud, a boy with an umbrella.

The words rise from the page like stormy weather:
pitch letters on the paper that come together,
a meaning system, an entire front worthy of civilization.

In his eyes, my student asks why third grade
is so hard? Why learning to read, decipher code is
demanded of him? In his mind, the black top
looms large, a flat surface for the scribble
of games, balls thrown, boys and girls giving chase.

We persevere, use our fingers against the literal
symbol of sound: c for cloud, s for storm, w for wind.
Slowly, just as tempests climb and brew,
he pulls away his hand, lifts the book,
proclaims the weather report,
all the verbs raining down.

Bingo

The Cherokee missing three teeth tells me
we were made in many colors, that all must be
present to fancy dance the world anew.

His plate is almost empty as I serve the cake,
red and yellow icing brightly splashing
the deep dark chocolate fill.

We've played bingo all evening: Tobias, twenty,
he's the dark fill. My white hands reach
for red buttons: I-14, G-39.

Across the table is Paul, the Indian, and at the end,
the Mexican kid who speaks no louder
than the blue teardrop stain upon his cheek.

In a space of two hours, in a room curtained
by unmatched donated sheets,
we amuse ourselves with games.

For a moment, I feel God's eye looking down,
hear a soft voice calling out while Oakland's soul
continues in its sleep:

B I N G O

Snapped Together

The corners of the jigsaw
do not matter much; we look for
the girl's hair split in two,
the place where a bunny ear
flops across cut lines.

I explain corners and flat edges,
point out the smooth distance
where the cardboard
turns into the horizon.

We settle pieces into borders,
meet odd angles, wavy lines.
The children are not impressed,
even as they name the animals
scattered across the yellow
fields, the earth-brown barnyard.

A red tractor rolls into view
at left of frame, a bucket spills
endless corn across the puzzle's
lower edge, underscoring
how these children live,
in old hotels at age three or five,
small seeds seeking soil
where they might have a chance
to take deeper root.

Briefly we work together,
the small boy, an older girl,
me, the childless volunteer
answering what questions
I can until we finally discover
the old but solid barn,
scattered plywood pieces
we snuggle into place.

In the neat snap — one, two, three —
we join the puzzle pieces
across the table's open space;
for awhile it covers
the stained vagrant rug
where kids plan
their future constructions.

Slaves, Prisoners, Artists

The Tug of Egypt

We all have our Egypts. Mine sprouts mirages
in old sand. Pressed into leaving, I see
tethered camels promised a quenched thirst.

In this night scented by Nile, our tombs
fill with sacrifice; still, this land
of first births is what I know. Some of us can't see

clear to leaving it, to wander
through a parted sea and storm of red,
for chance encounters with milk and manna.

I cling to Egypt the way a horse craves
its bridle, the way the nail brings the hammer down.
Why give up the solace of the lash,

the rudiments of bricklaying,
when what may lie in wait
is a land full of lizards and ravenous wasps?

Here are monuments we've etched in stone,
carved intricate wounds, statues
rinsed in brine; are these not gods made

visible and whole, who make the muck and mire
of floods seem burdens worth enduring?
I'm no Pharaoh, no visionary Joseph;

perhaps untimely deaths (starvations,
long days flicked by whips) are preferable
to a desert litany of stings and bruises.

Can we trust a covenant scratched out
on dust-blind roads by one who mutters?
This clutch of leather strap I hang on to

is a kind of comfort. Standing in a rain of locusts,
I wonder can the plagues be waited out
that come in droves?

And the bread. Our bread is not
yet risen, though I am being
urged to go.

Kidnap Song

Did they take us as we came down
to the water?
Our heads bowed to our reflections,
oval suns in blue-black
water.

Did they take what was best as we
kneeled to quench
our thirst?
The sweet fresh drink barely moistening
our tongues.

They took us in daylight, in dusk time, in dark
our sisters, our fathers.

Did they come in one fell swoop
like a vulture's wings,
or in fast ships to gather our pride
and our young
in nets made of nail and rust?

They took us in daylight, in dusk time, in dark
our mothers and brothers.

Did they take us by force with slip of a rope
or by promise of something
good to come?
Bowed to the pool, our hearts beating sound —
did they mean
to never
release us again?

Did they know, do they know what they
have done?

I Once Lived As a Tree Four Hundred Years

In that time, I saw ships come. They landed
on a shore so endless sweet until it bore
unseasonable fruit: cargoes of sea-salt
corpses, the dead asleep in bitter African sand.

Four hundred years I saw goings and comings,
unloading, whips, the auctioning of girls, chain-
bound feet. My roots drenched with weeping,
my own brown limbs bent through offering
another useless embrace. A mother watching
her son led away; tears were all she had left
after exhaustion. If I could have found a wind
to play through my branches, I might have
sung: "I can see your home from this great height."

I wanted to lay leaves across open sores as salve.
Instead, I shook with grief and let my budding stems
provide a shadow's cooling solace. When the last
debarked to take his place on an inland farm,
or was dropped back to take his turn at bone,
I carved my own rough skin with names until
a termite raid rotted me out to dust.

Plantation Pieces

I

Far from Eden, still our home on this red plantation clay
was once steadfast, a reason
for our worth, our mouthful of rage.
Now we stumble across the south, knapsacks wrapped
around what little we could carry:
change of clothes, a little roll, some candle sticks,
a wad of rope. My foot is heavy as I leave
so much behind; even the master's whip
that stings in my memory
also entwines with smells of biscuits burning,
a stolen moment's solace under greener oaks.
We launch ourselves again and again across an ocean
of strangers' hands who can only offer so much.
What we have: God's invisible protection,
a planted bond of hope.

II

I saw the sea of them bobbing in the distant light
as the shore of our slaked solitude rose up to take
their place. They moved as one body, dark song
of grief hanging in the cloud. Was it my doing
to bring this war, these years of pain, upon our tribe
of soured milk? I ponder now the gains, peruse
my fields, stained red, their blood, our babes.

You gave much, Old Man who sang in praise of rain,
up-heaving crops we shipped to far off land.
Bought our ladies' gowns, tobacco stained men's hands.
Why do they not look back as the horizon rises up
to meet their ship? I watch the sunset thread and catch
the masts; or are those whites I took for sails
just kerchiefs or the sacks they strapped on backs?

Song of the Slave Cheering the Punishment of One Caught

Ear tacked to a wood pole, then sliced off
Like watermelon, the strong man's
Head to explode in red and flesh.

He stumbles away in chains and the shout
Goes up, the lesson received and welcomed.

We won't run, master, we won't fight,
We won't harm your missus at midnight.

Standing in a pool of sweat and blood,
the proud scuffle away at last; the boldest
one among us stands like a beaten cur.

Lifts up his voice, "Amen! to his
come uppance." In the middle of the crowd
we scan the dirt below our feet
for the sharpest stones.

We won't run, master, we won't fight,
We won't come to rape your missus at midnight.

This scapegoat, the one about to receive
Five hundred lashes, be starved down to the bone,
is the proxy of us all, our Jesus whore.

For him we cheer the loudest, insisting
we be heard. And so shall it ever go,
the punishments of the poor.
We won't run, master, we won't fight,
We won't steel away your missus at midnight.

Slave Burying Ground

We came back through shadow and kudzu vine.
Tapping sticks on the leached ground, a bony
finger of wood our divining rod to reach
into such green confusion, to reach under, untangle,
reveal what's overgrown in this suffocating canopy.

We strike a rock, bend forward, set knees hard
on red clay packed dense by a century of leaves.
We lean in to the cool dark, an ancestor's unmarked
grave. A name shivers into light, a tan stone plate
appears and here's a female, another one's a man.

Gold struck among the rubble resting in a kind
of peace. With a glove we each wipe a tombstone
as clean as one extracted tooth, the wide white smile
of pelvic bone; clean as a white wave breaking
its own bent back on some stranger shore.

A shore dense and white as a cotton boll,
sharp as an unseen thorn.

Jail Librarian

First, there is the metal grate, then bars and pock-marked paint.
They roll on bunks, settle in grey blankets on metal cots.
Even the steel table is someone's bed.

Twelve, thirteen, I count them till the fight breaks out
over what's left of skim milk at the bottom of someone's cup.

The women scatter to the four corners of the concrete cell.
One grabs the monitor's broom; another flings paperbacks
just selected off my cart.

Trash piles flutter as the women scrap, wasted coffee
on a concrete floor seeps into the crack. I exit fast;

rhythm of a toilet flush, jangled chains of heavy keys
echo in my ears. One inmate squawks her last hurrah
at the cellmate she's just fought.

With my cart of books, I take the shorter path. Crossing
the courthouse plaza lawn there Lady Justice stands.

In summer's sunset haze, I've got just enough light
to inventory my stock: books on gangster love are gone,
but poetry too, and Plato and a Book of Psalms.

What's left behind, I carry back to my basement office:
fiction with unbent spines, and unthumbed tomes,

self-help books, the latest advice by writers who proffer
so much inspirational prose.

Hooker City

The prostitutes were her favorites.

Jail, their temporary home;
for most it was a place
of great relief: a break
from turning tricks,
battering pimps,
walking hot streets.

Some had tracks on their forearms,
bruised-blue constellations.
They laughed at the young librarian
who brought them books.

Through the bars, she slipped
light entertainment: *True Confessions*,
romance novels, books by Iceberg
Slim; she asked about their lives.

"Oh, if you could see our books,"
they teased, hinting at
names they had checked into
and out of their own
circulating libraries.

The girl couldn't mask her shock,
getting lessons in street cred, learning
how much was being done
to clean up Fresno's mean streets.

Shopping Cart House

Everywhere she goes
her plastic bags
go with her.
She is afraid
of the obvious camera.
Afraid of an unknown woman
scribbling notes
in her blank book
at the bus stop
just across.

Understand, she cannot
comprehend how
anyone could
make such a list
out of all
her miseries.

So Many Elijahs

There's the fellow on Fourth Street
who sits cross-legged on a faded
peach-colored blanket, his Fido
cradled in his lap. All day long,
he grooms the dog and manicures
its curled claws, paints them pink.

There's the black blind woman
who sells stolen newspapers; a can
jingles in one hand, white cane
in the other, stiff as a Moses rod.
In a wheelchair, another Elijah
shakes a plastic envelope. Inside
are hand-painted cards for sale.

There are Elijahs who haunt turn-
signal islands, Elijahs seeking
my support for a good cause
right out my screen-door.
It's never enough.

Elijahs seek recognition. I'm asked:
run and call the preacher, alert
the rabbi. Grab someone's sleeve,
tell them they must come see,
come see: the promise is fulfilled,
the world to come has come.

And I want to believe sure as sun's
gonna rise that Messiahs appear
in such lowly guise, more than in
any winged chariot enflamed.
The flaw is in me, who stands before
each Elijah, in a moment between
doing this or that, going here
or back to there, as when I glimpse
a blue light around the sallow garb.

Quick as it takes for me to turn
the lock or even to fall apart
while gazing into the Prophet's eyes . . .
before I see the way smoothed out
ahead of us, I move on. I move on.

Some Good for Society

After a public radio report about pharmaceutical trials on
"acres of skin" inside a Pennsylvania prison.

Paying my dues
for what I did.
I go to prison for
a lifetime or two.

Man in a white coat
comes with a stick,
takes skin,
leaves me cut,
and a dollar or two.

Hole in my arm,
salve it up, years
'til I feel it, long past
when harm's
been done.

Your ladies in blue
dressmaker's dresses,
waltzing at fundraisers,
well, they wear my skin
in pearlescent lotions.

You can say I did it
for the good of society,
all those bad tests
securing my legacy.

Don't pay no mind:
you can thank me
at my funeral.

The Aerialist

for Brendan Elms

Wendy wears red fringed
leotards and fishnet stockings,

climbing the white rope
like stairs to her apartment.

Up twenty feet she grabs
the trapeze, pulls herself up,

dangles mid-air with winds
scouring her skin.

She holds on to the rope
as if it were a ray of light,

so celestially serene upside-
down from sky tops,

feet entwined with ropes, until
she slips

ten inches down
a split second lasting forever.

Beyond the circus tent
the sun catches itself
at the ocean's edge.
No one sees it sink
into the other worlds
except a boy
who turned eight
just when the light winked
itself into the wide net
of an acrobatic sea.

The Impetuous Banjo Student

for Jody Stecher

The song that I came to sing remains unsung to this day. I have spent my days in stringing and unstringing my instrument. The time has not come true, the words have not been rightly set; only there is the agony of wishing in my heart. — from *Gitanjali* by Rabindranath Tagore

Driven forward by eagerness, I want
already to know, to have played
one hundred dance halls, padded the boards
in midsummer sweat.

I want to have sat
in endless night sessions on
brown splintered porches, iced tea
in a glass by my foot.

Now my music seems always
to miss. I steam ahead,
stumble past patience, thwart intuition,
lose the rail-car pulse

of Rufus Crisp, Wade Ward, Lilly Mae Ledford;
I go out to the limb,
the tender crook
of my limited understanding. Fingers jolt,

contradict the rhythm, muck up
the steady bum-ditty, bum-ditty dactyls
across the open air.
Yes, I could tune myself

more simply to accompany some
dirt-farmer's song but I came to this task
already adult, smug
in other accomplishments.

Acquisitive with learning, I handle it
rough, insult the gift through trials.
I'm always trying.

Inside the house, a woman tips back
in a red-rocking chair so chipped and carved,

worn as Appalachian hills;
I see her small knees eased apart,
her beat shoes tapping old ground.

I hear humming as she frails,
remembering all those words
that intertwine her song.

Door Harp

Appalachian roadside stand. She sells
what she can sew or make from fruit or wood.
No houses anywhere around. She comes
from the deep woods overgrown leaves under-growth
kudzu, vines around trunks, comes from
the dark inner nectar where she gathers
honey. Hives out of wind's way.
Smoke in the clearing. A rain bent
under passing glory clouds. She stirs
through the pines, her white muslin gown
torn by branch twines, barefoot slipped
over snakeskins, the fur of raccoon.
I stop on my way out of the city
because I must stop this headlong busy
ness settled in my chest like an old cold,
its march like General Sherman
on a treadmill to illusory ambition.
I buy one thing: a door harp of acacia wood,
old as the Bible, tune of my own
forgotten song.

For Edna

I was in your house; your cardigan
in the closet pink from an age
when women wore pink. You loved
once and often: you loved deep
as crumbling seas, swift as the thrush
who burst from view, soft as
your clinging magenta sweater.

Your page-boy lusts could not
help but love, so I have come
to your shrine to smell the talc, trace
a dusty path through milady's own
concoctions where I will roll
my right sleeve up to sweep
your cobwebbed wallpaper, release
the scent of summer petals.

It is mid-season in my own life,
my sweet and I need your
fearless way with bristlebush and rose,
your candlewax melted atop
a silver tray. I need the impatient
bed strewn with carnations, a nameless
lover parade, ashtray on a maple
bedstand beside chenille spread.

I need your conquest of stockings
doused in Chanel Number Infinity,
tossed in the extreme right unction
of your corner room, sweat smell
of bed-soaked pens to strike my flame.

About Art

Between sessions of *rond de jambe* and *grand jêté*,
five or six girls escape into the plaza. One knows
where a tiny nest holds pigeon eggs.

They gather on the far side of the stone
fountain that spires in the center of *Bellas Artes*,
a waterless rest break in an art school.

Their fearless leader, the taller girl in pink *tutu*
(the others wear black leotards, white tights)
dips a slender hand into the shadowed hedge:

Giggles become solemn sighs as they circle
a cup of leaves, observe the fading light,
drop knees to the nest settled on the ground.

Like tendons beneath torn flesh or a bleeding
row of toes on *pointe*, they contract,
one shoulder to shoulder to peer.

Confused little faces transform, disturbed
eyes wide, brown foreheads imprinted
by colored headbands holding back hair.

Meanwhile, the small alabaster lamb
atop the marble fountain retains
its muteness: it also knows

about sacrifice and the cracked egg
spilling the muddied life,
the wingless dove.

Inexhaustible

At the well, she drew water
from such blindness   I was seen
for what I am: a supplicant
in yellow robes, walking
alkali earth   in dusty devocation,
ululating like a
war-torn mother.

Her hand, a dark brown reed,
tended the crimson rope;
on each finger she wore
a golden band   to signal
she was lover to many
wife to One.   I watched her
pull with gentle force,
earth-fingers
laced around the cord   until
she let go.

The bucket pounded down —
lightning strike to pierce
the pool's most darkened deep.
I felt it strike the bottom:
an endless peal   yet, I heard how
it engaged the blow.

When our eyes met,   mine faltered:
I could not drink   her gaze.
Certain it had taken hold,
I saw the diamonds
of her breath,   smelled her fragrant
boundless heart.
With just one touch   yearning, full,
I felt her kiss me
            moistly
                once.

Notes to the Poems

About Art was inspired by a scene I witnessed at the Bellas Artes School in San Miguel de Allende, Mexico.

The Aerialist came from watching the Pickle Family Circus perform at Cedar-Rose Park in Berkeley on the occasion of my step-son's birthday.

Auto Commute Death of Teacher Who Maintained Second Job Site at Home was my response to typesetting a story in the *California Workers' Compensation Reporter* at a time when the state appeals board had become more restrictive in its application of workers' compensation benefits.

Earthquake, Taiwan, 1999. Unsound construction was blamed for the collapse of a building in Taiwan following this 7.6 earthquake which struck Taiwan, killing nearly 100 workers. Dissatisfaction in the government's response following the earthquake led to unseating the responsible political party in the nation's 2000 election.

Every Night She Swallows the Sun was inspired by a visit to the San Jose Rosicrucian Museum and seeing a ceiling painted in honor of an Egyptian goddess whose cycle represented the setting of the sun and rising of the moon.

Express Market, Starbucks, Grace Beauty Supply, East Bay Rats, and *Police Training Unit* are poems prompted by things seen while walking or taking the bus to and from work in Oakland; for eight years I worked as a typographer and am fascinated by fonts and the language of printing.

For Edna was inspired by Edna St. Vincent Millay.

Inexhaustible is an imaginative encounter with the *shekheina*, the feminine manifestation of God in Judaism. Some may read it as a poem of lesbian love; that is fine with me too.

Jail Librarian and *Hooker City* both come from an early job experience working in the corrections project for Fresno County Library; it was a job constantly under threat of being cut. "Hooker City" is the tag for Fresno that many truckers used in the 1970s.

Kidnap Song was inspired by a photograph of antelope bending to a drinking hole in Africa.

La Llorona (The Weeping Woman) is based on a Mexican legend of a ghostly woman who mourns beside a river for her dead children. Some say it goes back to the Conquest of the Aztecs by Cortés and his Aztec paramour, La Malinche.

Lowell and *Poe at Lowell* are poems resulting from my interest in early American textile workers; Lowell, Massachusetts was America's first planned industrial town. With a large population of Yankee farm girls in its work force, there was a ready population for visiting writers and lecturers during a time in the early 1800's when educating the masses seemed like a good idea in our new democratic republic.

Mortician's After Hours is one of those strange poems that arrive in dreams, that cannot be explained or tied to daytime reality.

The Packing House in Clovis, California, was my first job out of high school.

Plantation Pieces came from an exercise I assigned to my East Oakland class on African-American poetry which was to write a poem from the point of view of a newly freed slave, and from the point of view of a slave-owner told he must now free his slaves following the Emancipation Proclamation.

Rebel Rebel was a hit song for David Bowie in 1974 when I worked in a chain record store in Fresno. New hires were required to undergo lie-detector tests; even the young women applying for work were sent to meet a strange man in a motel room where the testing was being done.

Song of the Slave Cheering the Punishment of One Caught is my effort to dramatize a true story that I read about in a history of the abominations of slavery.

Typhoon. Cyclone Nargis was the worst national disaster in Burma, striking land in May 2008, causing over 138,000 deaths when waters reaching 40 kilometers swooshed up the Irawaddy Delta. There were allegations that the Burmese government stopped counting fatalities to avoid political fall-out. Political leaders there resisted international aid, worsening the impact.

Words Under Fingertips, *Bingo*, and *Snapped Together* grew from experiences as a volunteer in homeless and transitional-housing shelters in downtown Oakland, California.

Acknowledgments

To wonderful teachers: Mrs. Carstens who taught me how to read; Mrs. Michaelis who taught me how to learn (Easterby Elementary School, Fresno); Carol Sarkisian (journalism teacher, Roosevelt High School, Fresno); poetry teachers Peter Everwine, Theresa Bacon, Mary Webb, Chana Bloch, Diana O'Hehir, David Wagoner and Al Young.

To my production partners in making this book, especially the exquisitely talented Margaret Copeland, the patient and kind Fred Fassett, and photographer Michele Scotto Trani.

To fellow poets and poetry students who have helped me become a better writer, especially Jan Barlow, Robert Coats, Rafaella Del Bourgo, Lawrence DiCostanzo, Marc Hofstadter, David Kolodney, Dan Marlin, Anita May, Adam David Miller, Gail Peterson, Jeannette Perez, Connie Soper, Sharon Jocelyn Waller, and Diane Wang.

To the few good bosses I have known: Dan Crosby (B. Dalton Bookstore, Fresno), Bill Houk (Fresno County Library, Corrections Project), Rick Heide (Archetype Typography), Alice Pasqualetti (Cat Companion Care), Mel Witt (California Workers' Compensation Reporter), Michele Taggert (Cody's Books), and Thaddea Pojanowska.

To wonderful friends and family.

Most of all, to my beloved husband, Julian López-Morillas, who continues to provide an example of a true artist supremely dedicated to his craft.

Publication Credits

The following poems were previously published:

"Auto Commute Death of Teacher Who Maintained Second Job Site at Home." *California Workers' Compensation Reporter*, edited by Melvin Witt (Berkeley, CA).

"Greetings from the Vogue Accessory Director." *Bakunin, Vol. 2* (Simi Valley, CA:1991).

"La Migra." Benicia Art Program: "I Read the News Today," featuring poetry and art, Benicia Public Library, under direction by Ronna Leon, 2011.

"Libby." *Across the Generations, Vol. VII*, publication of Vista Community College, Berkeley, California, under the direction of Marcy Alancraig, 1988.

"Mortician's After Hours." *Riverbabble* online literary journal, edited by Leila Rae, 2012.

"The Packing House." *Americas Review* (Berkeley, CA 1989).

"What the Children Saw." *Sunrust* (Dawn Valley Press, New Wilmington, PA:1989).

About the Author

Jannie M. Dresser is a San Francisco Bay Area poet with roots in the San Joaquin Valley. She has worked at a wide variety of jobs throughout her life, many of which are evidenced in these poems.

She has written poetry and articles for over forty years, and teaches poetry, creative writing, and basic writing skills. She helped co-found a literacy project that continues to serve Oakland public school children. She co-founded and published the *Bay Area Poets Seasonal Review* for seven years and currently leads salons in three Bay Area cities where people share their love of language and poetry. In 2012, she created Sugartown Publishing to help writers get their work into attractive print and electronic media.

She is married to Shakespeare scholar and veteran Bay Area theater actor, Julian López-Morillas. They live in Crockett, California, where the Sierra Nevada rivers stream in from the valley to feed the San Francisco Bay.

Colophon

The font used in this book is primarily Goudy Old Style, an old-style classic serif typeface originally created by Frederic W. Goudy for American Type Founders (ATF) in 1915. The following fonts are used in the poems on pages 114–118: **Arial Black**, *Snell Roundhand*, 𝕰𝖓𝖌𝖑𝖎𝖘𝖍𝖊 𝕿𝖔𝖜𝖓𝖊, and American Typewriter.

Thee do I crave co-partner in that verse
Which I presume on Nature to compose...
Divine one, give my words
Immortal charm.
— *Lucretius, 50 BCE, De Rerum Natura*

Sugartown Publishing

Based in Crockett, California, home to the famous C&H Sugar plant.

SUGARTOWN PUBLISHING JOINED A LONG-ESTABLISHED TRADITION OF
COOPERATIVE PUBLISHING IN **2012.** We are dedicated to bringing into
print, electronic and audio media formats *works of literary merit that have
something significant to say.*

Current and forthcoming titles include:

A Stalwart Bends, Poems and Reflections, by Ben Slomoff (2012).
Doing Time With Nehru, memoir by Yin Marsh (2012).
Among the Shapes that Fold and Fly, poetry by Patricia Nelson (2013).
Between the Fault Lines: Eight East Bay Poets, edited by Jannie M. Dresser (2013).
Workers' Compensation: Poems of Labor & the Working Life, by Jannie M. Dresser (2013).
Swimming the Sky, poetry by Gail Peterson (2013).
It Lasts a Moment: New & Collected Poems, by Fred Ostrander (2013).
Falling Home, poetry by Gary Turchin (2013).
Voices from the Field, poetry by Kimberly Satterfield (2013).
At My Table, poetry by Judith Yamamoto (2013).
Stronger than I Know, inspirational poetry from Cheri Coleman (2014).
The Glass Ship, prose-poems by Judy Wells (2014).
Yew Nork, poetry by Dale Jensen (2014).

Contact us for more information on how we can help you get your book into print.

sugartownpublishing.com
janniedres@att.net
Mailing address:
1164 Solano Ave. #140,
Albany, CA 94706